KU-072-147

Evelyn Waugh was born in Hampstead in 1903, second son of Arthur Waugh, publisher and literary critic, and brother of Alec Waugh, the popular novelist. He was educated at Lancing and Hertford College, Oxford, where he read Modern History. In 1928 he published his first work, a life of Dante Gabriel Rossetti, and his first novel, *Decline and Fall*, which was soon followed by *Vile Bodies* (1930), *Black Mischief* (1932), *A Handful of Dust* (1934), and *Scoop* (1938). During these years he travelled extensively in most parts of Europe, the Near East, Africa, and tropical America and published a number of travel books including *Labels* (1930), *Remote People* (1931), *Ninety-two Days* (1934) and *Waugh in Abyssinia* (1936). In 1939 he was commissioned in the Royal Marines and later transferred to the Royal Horse Guards, serving in the Middle East and in Yugoslavia. In 1942 he published *Put Out More Flags* and then in 1945 *Brideshead Revisited*. *When the Going Was Good* and *The Loved One* preceded *Men At Arms*, which came out in 1952, the first volume of 'The Sword of Honour' trilogy, and won the James Tait Black Memorial Prize. The other volumes, *Officers and Gentlemen* and *Unconditional Surrender*, followed in 1955 and 1961. *The Ordeal of Gilbert Pinfold* appeared in 1957, the *Life of Ronald Knox* in 1959 and *A Little Learning*, Waugh's last book and the first volume of a projected autobiography, in 1964. Evelyn Waugh was received into the Roman Catholic Church in 1930 and his biography of the Elizabethan Jesuit martyr, *Edmund Campion*, was awarded the Hawthornden Prize in 1936. For many years he lived with his wife and six children in the West Country. He died in 1966.

Waugh said of his work: 'I regard writing not as investigation of character but as an exercise in the use of language, and with this I am obsessed. I have no technical psychological interest. It is drama, speech and events that interest me.' Mark Amory called Evelyn Waugh 'one of the five best novelists in the English language this century', while Harold Acton described him as having 'the sharp eye of a Hogarth alternating with that of the Ancient Mariner'.

M/Y STELLA POLARIS, 1929

Frontispiece

PENGUIN BOOKS

Published by the Penguin Group
Penguin Books Ltd, 80 Strand, London WC2R 0RL, England
Penguin Putnam Inc., 375 Hudson Street, New York, New York 10014, USA
Penguin Books Australia Ltd, Ringwood, Victoria, Australia
Penguin Books Canada Ltd, 10 Alcorn Avenue, Toronto, Ontario, Canada M4V 3B2
Penguin Books (NZ) Ltd, 182–190 Wairau Road, Auckland 10, New Zealand

Penguin Books Ltd, Registered Offices: 80 Strand, London WC2R 0RL, England

First published by Gerald Duckworth and Company Ltd
Published in Penguin Books 1985

8

Brief references to photographs which are no longer
available have been omitted on p. 147.

Printed in Great Britain by Clays Ltd, St Ives plc
Filmset in 10/12½pt Monophoto Baskerville

ISBN 978-0-140-18837-0

www.greenpenguin.co.uk

MIX
Paper from
responsible sources
FSC
www.fsc.org   FSC™ C018179

Penguin Books is committed to a sustainable
future for our business, our readers and our
planet. This book is made from paper certified
by the Forest Stewardship Council.

Evelyn Waugh

LABELS

A Mediterranean Journal

Penguin Books

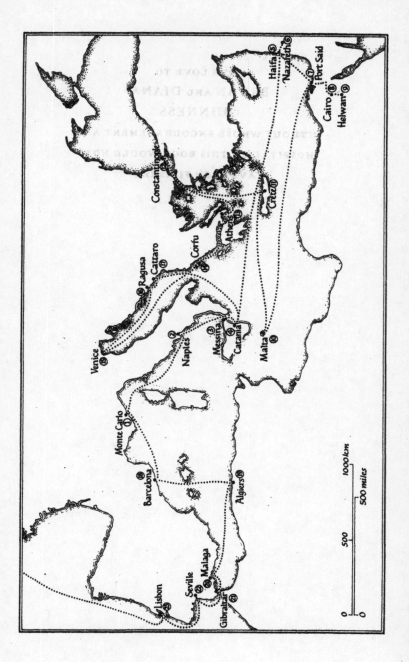

ONE

I did not really know where I was going, so, when anyone asked me, I said to Russia. Thus my trip started, like an autobiography, upon a rather nicely qualified basis of falsehood and self-glorification. The statement cannot be held to be wholly deceptive because it was potentially true, and also it was made without any informative motive at all. I wanted to go to Russia very much, and someone once persuaded me that, if you went on for long enough saying that you would go somewhere, you always got there eventually. For the fortnight before I left England and for as long after that as I was heading east, I kept saying I was going to Russia; I told three gossip-writers of my intention and they printed it in their papers; I told a very polite young man at Cook's office that I was going there and wasted a great deal of his time in looking up steamship routes in the Black Sea; I even, provisionally and with many cautious reservations, booked a passage from Constanza to Odessa and obtained letters of introduction to people who were reputed to have influence with the Soviet Embassy at Angora. But the spell did not work; I never got nearer to Russia than the eastern mouth of the Bosphorus.

I do not suppose that the self-glorification did me very much good either; that is a part of the business of writing which I have not fully mastered. I suppose that by the time this book is published it will be quite a common and simple thing to go to Russia for a holiday. At the time of which I am writing – February 1929 – there was a Conservative majority in the House of Commons and it was a very adventurous project indeed. Now, one of the arts of successful authorship is preventing the reading public from forgetting one's name in between the times when they are reading one's books. It is all very puzzling because, as far as I can see, there are only two respectable reasons for reading a book written by someone else; one

7

is that you are being paid to review it, and the other that you are continually meeting the author and it seems rude not to know about him. But clearly there are masses of people to whom neither of these reasons apply. They read books because they have heard the author's name. Now, even if you are very industrious, you cannot rely on writing more than two books a year, which will employ your public, as it is called, for about six hours each. That is to say, that for every hour in which you employ your reader's attention, you are giving her a month to forget you. It would be very difficult to organize even a marriage on that basis, still more one's financial career. So you have to spend half your leisure in writing articles for the papers; the editors buy these because people read your books, and people read your books because they see your articles in the papers. (This is called a vicious circle by those who have not got into the running.) The rest of your leisure you have to spend in doing things which you think other people will think interesting. My hope was that, when someone saw in the gossip page that I was going to Russia, she would say, what a very interesting young man, and, I must get his life of Dante Gabriel Rossetti out of the circulating library. Well, even this did not happen to any appreciable extent, so I must begin this book, which is going to aim at what the reviewers call the uncompromising sincerity and frankness of youth, by admitting that the whole lie was a flop.

However, I did succeed in getting away from England, and that was all I really cared about. In February 1929 almost every cause was present which can contribute to human discomfort. London was lifeless and numb, seeming to take its temper from Westminster, where the Government, conscious of failure, was dragging out the weeks of its last session. Talking films were just being introduced, and had set back by twenty years the one vital art of the century. There was not even a good murder case. And besides this it was intolerably cold. The best seller of the preceding months had been Mrs Woolf's *Orlando*, and it seemed almost as though Nature were setting out to win some celestial Hawthornden Prize by imitation of that celebrated description of the Great Frost. People shrank, in those days, from the icy contact of a cocktail glass, like the Duchess of Malfi from the dead hand, and crept stiff as automata from their draughty taxis into the nearest tube railway station, where they stood, pressed

8

together for warmth, coughing and sneezing among the evening papers. Intense cold seems peculiarly insupportable in a great city, where one's converse with the seasons is wholly capricious and unrelated to the natural processes of germination and decay.

So I packed up all my clothes and two or three very solemn books, such as Spengler's *Decline of the West*, and a great many drawing materials, for two of the many quite unfulfilled resolutions which I made about this trip were that I was going to do some serious reading and drawing. Then I got into an aeroplane and went to Paris.

I had been up before. During what proved to be my last term at Oxford, an ex-officer of the R.A.F. appeared in Port Meadow with a very dissolute-looking Avro biplane, and advertised passenger flights for seven and sixpence or fifteen shillings for 'stunting'. On a very serene summer evening I went for a 'stunt' flight. It was a memorable experience. Some of the movements merely make one feel dizzy, but 'looping the loop' develops in the mind clearly articulated intellectual doubts of all preconceived habits of mind about matter and movement. There used to be a very terrifying thing at Wembley called the Great Racer. 'Looping the loop' is that thing prolonged to its logical extreme. There were moments on the Great Racer, when the car was in full flight, during which one's nerves reached the highest point of excitement, trembling between ordinary healthy terror and mad panic. Just at that zenith of emotion the car always slackened in speed or changed its direction, so that a few seconds of comparative calm were interspersed between the successive crises. In 'looping', the aeroplane shoots steeply upwards until the sensation becomes unendurable and one knows that in another moment it will turn completely over. Then it keeps on shooting up and does turn completely over. One looks down into an unfathomable abyss of sky, while over one's head a great umbrella of fields and houses have suddenly opened. Then one shuts one's eyes. My companion on this occasion was a large-hearted and reckless man; he was President of the Union, logical, matter-of-fact in disposition, inclined towards beer and Ye Olde Merrie Englande, with a marked suspicion and hostility towards modern invention. He had come with me in order to assure himself that it was really all nonsense about things heavier than air being able to fly. He sat behind me throughout, muttering, 'Oh, my God, oh, Christ, oh, my

God.' On the way back he scarcely spoke, and two days later, without a word to anyone, he was received into the Roman Church. It is interesting to note that, during this aeroplane's brief visit to Oxford, three cases of conversion occurred in precisely similar circumstances. I will not say that this aeronaut was directly employed by Campion House, but certainly, when a little later he came down in flames, the Jesuits lost a good ally, and to some people it seemed as if the Protestant God had asserted supremacy in a fine Old Testament manner.

My flight to Paris was not at all like this. It was disagreeable but quite unexciting. I was taken with one other passenger in a charabanc from the London office to Croydon. The ticket seemed very cheap until they weighed my luggage and got me to understand how much there was to pay. Then I wished I was going by train. The other passenger was a smartly dressed woman of early middle age; she had only a small attaché case with her. We got into conversation in the charabanc. She said she made this journey on business every week. She was in business in Paris. When you were very busy with business it saved time to fly. I suppose business women never get bored with the idea of their being business women. It is an adventure all the time.

The charabanc took us to a large station with a waiting-room and ticket office, a buffet and a passport officer and a bookstall. It was rather a surprise to leave this building and find a grass field and a huge aeroplane. The business woman and I climbed up a ladder into the aeroplane. It was not the newest sort because they are more expensive. Low wicker armchairs were arranged on each side of a narrow gangway. At the back was a funny little lavatory. The floor sloped steeply uphill when the machine was on the ground. The windows were small and filled with sliding panes of glass. These, I discovered when we started, kept opening of their own accord through the vibration. The body of the aeroplane was built over the planes, so that we could not see out very easily.

The pilot and the mechanic got in, and we started our flight. Although, presumably, we were travelling a great deal faster than the old Avro in Port Meadow, there was practically no sensation of speed. We seemed to float along in the gentlest way possible. The only movement of which I was conscious was the sudden dropping into air pockets, and this was sensible to the stomach rather than the eye. The chief discomforts of air travelling were, I discovered, those which had drawn me from London, only intensified very severely – cold and noise. The roar of the propellers was shattering. I followed the advice of the company and put cotton wool in my ears, but even so had a headache for some hours afterwards. The cold is worst about one's feet, which are provided with fur-lined footbags. The things which amused me most were (1) the spectacle of a completely horizontal rain storm, and (2) of the pilot telephoning our positions (it seemed extraordinary that they could hear him at Le Bourget when we could scarcely hear him within a few feet), and (3) the look of frightful scorn on the face of the business woman when, soon after we left Le Touquet, I was sick into the little brown paper bag provided for me. One does not feel nearly as ill being airsick as seasick; it is very much more sudden and decisive, but I was acutely embarrassed about my bag. If we had been over the channel it would have been different, but I could not bring myself to throw it out of the window over the countryside. In the end I put it down the little lavatory. As this opened directly into the void the effect was precisely the same, but my conscience was easier in the matter.

The view was fascinating for the first few minutes we were in the air and after that very dull indeed. It was fun to see houses and motor cars looking so small and neat; everything had the air of having been made very recently, it was all so clean and bright. But after a very short time one tires of this aspect of scenery. I think it is significant that a tower or a high hill are all the eminence one needs for observing natural beauties. All one gains from this effortless ascent is a large scale map. Nature, on an elusive principle, seems usually to provide its own viewpoints where they are most desirable. The Citadel at Cairo, or Canoni Point at Corfu, or the top of the mountain road above Cattaro, lose nothing at all of their supremacy from the knowledge that we can now always go higher if we want to, but, on the contrary, seem rather to gain by their peculiar fitness and adequacy. There was one sight, however, which was unforgettable – that of Paris lying in a pool of stagnant smoke, looking, except for the Eiffel Tower, very much like High Wycombe indefinitely extended. After the exaggerated cleanliness and sparkle of the preceding country, this exaggerated sombreness and squalor, called up (particularly to me, who had lately been sick) all the hatred and weariness which the modern megalopolitan sometimes feels towards his own civilization.

Then we saw below us the aerodrome of Le Bourget, marked out as though for some game. The aeroplane went far beyond it, and only the obvious calmness of the business woman, who closed with a snap the little notebook which she had been filling with sums during the journey, reassured me that we were not being misled. Then we turned round, banking over and descending rapidly, till it seemed as though our wing must catch on the top of the hangars; then a slight bumping and a feeling of buoyancy proclaimed that we were on the ground; we ran forward more slowly and came to rest in front of the station. Here our passports and luggage were examined and we were transferred to a charabanc, which presently deposited us and our luggage in the middle of Paris at the very inconvenient hour when everyone has just finished his luncheon.

There were several friends in Paris whom I wanted to see, but at the moment I did not feel up to coping with telephones or *concierges*; nor did I feel inclined to start looking for rooms; so, rather extravagantly, I drove to the Crillon. I asked for the cheapest bedroom and bathroom they had. There was a very nice little one for 180 francs, said the man at the reception counter. I said I wanted a cheaper one. He said I could have the same room for 140, so I took it. It was, as he said, very nice, with plenty of electric lights and cupboards and a comfortable bed. But I did not really feel I was abroad at all. When one has got accustomed to a certain kind of approach – the trains and boats and queues and customs and crowd – a new route seems very unconvincing. So I undressed, had a very hot bath, and went to sleep. It was not until I woke up and found it was quite dark that I really felt that I was in Paris. Then I ordered some tea and began telephoning from my bed.

I need hardly say that directly I felt strong enough, which was before noon next day, I left the Crillon for cheaper accommodation. My next hotel was remarkably less comfortable. It was exactly facing into the Metro, where it runs very noisily above ground, and the bed was, I think, stuffed with skulls. The only furniture was a bidet and a cupboard full of someone else's underclothes. There were some false teeth under the pillows, and the door opened oddly, being permanently locked and detached from both hinges, so that it could only be moved at the wrong side just far enough to admit of one squeezing through. However, it was cheaper than the Crillon, costing in fact only 18 francs a night. I was rescued from here after a night or two and removed to the cheapest way of living of all – as a guest in a seventeenth-century apartment near the Quai d'Orsay. I stayed in Paris altogether about ten days before moving on south.

Now, Paris is a very well-known city – next to Rome, I suppose, the best-known in the world – and it is one which has come to bear all kinds of romantic labels for all kinds of people. I have called this book *Labels* for the reason that all the places I visited on this trip are already fully labelled. I was no adventurer of the sort who can write books with such names as *Off the Beaten Track in Surrey* or *Plunges into Unknown Herts*. I suppose there is no track quite so soundly beaten as the Mediterranean seaboard; no towns so constantly and completely overrun with tourists as those I intend to describe. But the interest I have found in preparing this book, which I hope may be shared by some of its readers, was that of investigating with a mind as open as the English system of pseudo-education allows, the basis for the reputations these famous places have acquired.

The characteristic thing about Paris is not so much the extent – though that is vast – as the overwhelming variety of its reputation. It has become so overlaid with successive plasterings of paste and proclamation that it has come to resemble those rotten old houses one sometimes sees during their demolition, whose crumbling frame of walls is only held together by the solid strata of wallpapers.

What, after all these years, can we say about Paris? There is a word, 'bogus', which I have heard used a great deal with various and often inconsistent implications. It seems to me that this scrap of jargon, in every gradation of meaning, every innuendo, every allusion and perversion and 'bluff' it is capable of bearing, gives a very adequate expression of the essence of modern Paris.

Paris is bogus in its lack of genuine nationality. No one can feel a foreigner in Monte Carlo, but Paris is cosmopolitan in the diametrically opposite sense, that it makes everyone a foreigner. London, deficient as it is in all the attributes which make a town habitable, is, at least, British. It is our own family skeleton in our own cupboard. Bath and Wells and Birmingham are all implicit in

London in a way in which Tours or Tarascon or Lyons are not implicit in Paris; the febrile ardours of French political life, the tenacity and avarice and logic and militancy of French character, seem out of place and improbable in the French capital. And sensitive Frenchmen confess to a feeling of awkwardness there. In England and Germany and the United States people flock to the great towns because they do express the life of the country. London is squalid and coarse, but Englishmen can feel at ease there, as, no doubt, they would still feel at ease in revisiting their homes, even though their mother drank and the butler had fits in the dining-room. Parisians, except the wealthy and elegant, have their eyes for the most part turned away from Paris. When they have collected enough tips they will buy some land in the country and play dominoes in the evening at the chief café of a provincial town. It is in Paris that money must be made, but is best spent in the provinces. They are stuck there for the time being, and impatient to get away. Sometimes in the evening, when the shops and offices are just closing and the Americans are beginning to file into the cocktail bars, I have stood in the Place de la Concorde, attempting vainly to attract a taxi, and seen the whole of Paris like one traffic jam, imprisoned by the increasing confluence of vehicles, and every horn trumpeting for release.

The fiction of Paris, conceived by Hollywood and the popular imagination, seems yearly to impose its identity more and more as the real city of Richelieu and Napoleon and Verlaine fades into the distance. This fictitious city expresses itself in dress parades, studios, and night clubs.

The first of these, because it is modern and commercialized, seems to me by far the most interesting. There is an inscrutable world, of which one occasionally catches a tantalizing glimpse or reflection, behind the industry of making women's clothes, which seems to promise, to anyone happy enough to penetrate into that close society, a rich and almost virgin literary soil. The high diplomacy of the *couturiers*; the espionage of the *copistes*; the wicked senators' wives who smuggle their maids into the mannequin shows; the secrets and intrigues and betrayals in the *ateliers*; the simple private lives of mannequins and *vendeuses*; the genius who lives in an attic and conceives robes he will never see for beautiful women he will never meet; the great designer who steals his ideas; the life of the frock as its character is shaped and modified and enriched by the impact of each personality through whose mind it passes; its eventual emergence into reality – what a world to sack! One of the acute problems of authorship today is to find any aspect of social organization about which one can get down one's seventy thousand words without obvious plagiarism; novelists are driven to stake out their own countries or counties, preserving a squatter's right upon Sussex farms, or high society, or sailors or tropical ne'er-do-wells or black men or pirates; or they hunt for improbable themes of women turned into foxes, or men who live for centuries and finally turn into women, or about little children who commit murder. Why not a novel in which the heroine is a dress, instead of its wearer?

That Paris shall be the centre of this enticing world is simply one of the accidents of commercial organization; talent and reputation find it convenient to concentrate there. There is nothing essentially modish in the atmosphere of Paris, any more than there is anything specifically medical in the atmosphere of Harley Street. In almost all matters except the business of dressmaking, Parisian taste is notably lower and less progressive than Berlin or Vienna or even London. The French, through the defects rather than the qualities of their taste, are saved from the peculiarly English horrors of folk dancing, arts and crafts, and the collection of cottage antiquities, only to fall victim, one false thing driving out another, to the worst sort of sham modernity. If the choice is inevitable between pewter-*cum*-warming-pan-*cum*-timbered-gables and the glass of M. Lalique, it is surely better to be imposed upon by a past which one has not seen than by a present of which one is oneself a part? The hand of M. Lalique is heavy on Paris, and oh, those iridescent balls at *Le Boeuf sur le Toit*!

During my visit to Paris I drove to see the Rue Mallet Stevens, which was then still under construction. It is a poignant example of the Parisian aptitude for missing the point of an artistic impulse. Confronted by that dismal metamorphosis of the German bourgeois utilitarian ideal into terms of Parisian *chic*, I felt very proud of the Underground stations of the London suburbs.

Then there is the Trilby tradition, still a vital reality in popular imagination. How many hearts still beat faster beneath paint-smudged pinafores at the thought of this life of artistic activity! But Paris never, even in the very glorious eighties, quite succeeded in getting painting under its full control. Sincere attempts are always being made to organize the art market, like dress designing, on strictly commercial lines, but here considerations other than mere mode and scarcity keep obtruding themselves. There is gambling among art dealers, and genuine enthusiasm, and incidentally Paris is one of the most difficult towns of Europe in which to sell a painting. Paris always just fails to standardize the fashion in art. It does, however, succeed in fostering experiment. There are preposterous pictures in Paris as there are not preposterous frocks, but there is also the possibility of discovery. In this hope I spent a chilly morning in the Rue de la Boëthie, going from exhibition to exhibition, but was confronted everywhere by a deadly predominance of those two Laliques of paintings Laurencin and Foujita. There was a more entertaining exhibition across the river, organized by M. Waldemar George in the Rue Bonaparte. He called it, I think quite justly, a 'Panorama of Contemporary Art'. It was very French. Picabia and Ernst hung cheek by jowl; these two abstract pictures, the one so defiant and chaotic, probing with such fierce intensity into every crevice and convolution of negation, the other so delicately poised, so impossibly tidy, discarding so austerely every accident, however agreeable, that could tempt disorder, seemed between them to typify the continual conflict of modern society. There were some decorative canvases whose counterparts I was later to see at Cnossos. There was a picture in which the paint was moulded in low relief. In a corner, displayed before black velvet curtains, hung the apotheosis of bogosity – a head made in white wire, so insignificant in form and character, so drab and boring and inadequate that it suggested the skeleton of a phrenologist's bust. The workmanship was fairly neat, and resembled in many ways the kind of barely ingenious handicraft pursued in hospitals by the disabled, who are anxious to employ their fingers without taxing their intellect or senses. It was called *Tête: dessin dans l'espace*, by M. Jean Cocteau; near it stood a magnificent sculpture by Maillol.

In an exhibition of such gross and almost wanton catholicity, claiming to represent *une action impartiale mais point neutre, orientée vers les formes qu'à défaut d'autres termes on qualifie de modernes, de vivantes*, I was proud to observe that my country, too, was not unrepresented, for there on the table among so much that was perplexing and disconcerting, I was delighted to find a prettily decorated edition of the poems of Mr Humbert Wolfe.

But it is not with M. Poiret or M. Cocteau that most people associate the name of Paris. Wherever *La Vie Parisienne* circulates – furtively smuggled from hand to hand in public schools, stickily thumbed in messes and club rooms in remote quarters of the globe – there are good young men saving up their money for a beano in 'Gay Paree'. And certainly some honour is due to the organizers of Paris night life. Montmartre is a kind of Wembley Exhibition of what anyone has at any time ever thought to be at all pleasurable. Even the ordinary pseudo-respectable round of night clubs – Ciro's, Florence's, the Plantation, Shéherazade, the Grand Ecart, and the rest – are not quite wholly dismal. One cannot help noticing that their patrons look scarcely half as bored as they do in London, and on consideration I found three good reasons for this partial absence of gloom. One is that a great many of those one sees round one are destitute Russians and Viennese who are paid to sit there and look gay; another is that there are so many other places to go on to that one escapes that claustrophobia one is liable to in London, when one's host has signed one in and paid vast guest fees and one knows he is there for the next two hours without hope of release; another is that lots of people are tipsy.

It is one of the modern pseudodoxia epidemica that 'you never see a drunk man in France'. As a race, it is true, the French tend to have strong heads, weak stomachs, and a rooted abhorrence of hospitality. But it is a revelation to see the Paris-Americans drink. The difference between them and the English makes an interesting example of the effects of legislation on appetite. Every true-born Briton lives under a fixed persecution mania that someone is always trying to prevent him from getting a drink. Of course, this is true, but the significant thing is how little they have succeeded. They have been at it now for nearly a hundred and fifty years, and it is still the easiest thing in the world to get drunk in England, and, if that is what is desired, to remain drunk for weeks at a time. (A far more just cause of complaint, which I commend to the Ye-Olde-Merrie-Englande School of grumblers, is that someone is always trying to put us to

17

bed.) If one wishes to drink in London it is possible, by acquainting oneself with the vagaries of the licensing laws, to do so without resorting to any more underhand means than passing oneself off as a bona fide market porter, for eighteen hours in the twenty-four. If this dull intervening period is spent on a travelling railway train with restaurant or pullman accommodation, one can fill one's whole life with a happy round of toping. However, the Merrie-Englanders have so eloquently upheld the cause of freedom that a subdued but smouldering resentment is now one of our national characteristics. Once the Englishman abroad has fully assured himself of the fact that he can buy wine or beer or spirits whenever he wants them, it is usual to see him adopting the routine to which he is accustomed. He does not rise up early in the morning to follow after strong drink, or deny himself his usual allowance of sleep for the delight of quaffing some champagne after bedtime. Not so the Americans, to whom each new bottle comes with an aura of fresh romance. They endow the ancient and prosaic business of wine-selling with the glamour the Englishman reserves for the ancient and prosaic business of brothel-keeping. It is these dazzled Americans, and not only the tourists but the residents, who keep the night life of Paris going.

The thing which chiefly distinguishes the night life of Paris from that of London is that it can be indefinitely prolonged and almost indefinitely varied. But even in its wide variety, there breaks in on one's appreciation the still small voice of the débutante, whispering 'bogus'.

I spent a night with some kind, generous, and wholly delightful Americans. They wanted to show me a place called 'Brick-Top's', which was then very popular. We dined at Ciro's, where the food was delicious and the clientele almost unmixed American. It was no good going to Bricky's, they said, until after twelve, so we went to Florence's first. We drank champagne because it is one of the peculiar modifications of French liberty that one can drink nothing else. Florence's was full of what apparently were well-known people, and here I was introduced to a snobbery that was new to me and is, as far as I have seen, quite unknown in London; that is, the hierarchy of the high demi-monde, the kept women of very rich men, who are all famous, and, without having any social position or set of friends, are able to make the reputation for smartness of dress shops and restaurants. I modestly greeted a few simple and shabby acquaintances of my own while these celebrities were being pointed out to me.

Then we went to an underground public house called the New York Bar. When we came in all the people beat on the tables with little wooden hammers, and a young Jew who was singing made a joke about the ermine coat which one of our party was wearing. We drank some more, much nastier, champagne and went to Brick-Top's, but when we got there, we found a notice on the door saying, 'Opening at four. Bricky', so we started again on our rounds.

We went to a café called *Le Fétiche*, where the waitresses wore dinner-jackets and asked the ladies in the party to dance. I was interested to see the fine, manly girl in charge of the cloakroom very deftly stealing a silk scarf from an elderly German.

We went to the Plantation, where the paintings on the walls are first rate, and to the Music Box, where it was so dark we could hardly see our glasses (which contained still nastier champagne), and to Shéherazade, where the waiters are very impressive. They brought us five different organs of lamb spitted together between onions and bay leaves, all on fire at the end and very nice to eat.

We went to Kasbek which was just like Shéherazade.

Finally, at four, we went to Brick-Top's, a really intimate and delightful negro cabaret. Brick-Top came and sat at our table. She seemed the least bogus person in Paris. It was broad daylight when we left; then we drove to the Halles and ate fine, pungent onion soup at Le Père Tranquille, while one of the young ladies in our party bought a bundle of leeks and ate them raw. I asked my host if all his evenings were like this. He said, no, he made a point of staying at home at least one night a week to play poker.

Now all this is recorded, not to show what a devil of a fellow I am when I am on the spree, but to make clear my point about bogosity, because all this feverish gumping from place to place would be justifiable, and indeed admirable, if each excursion, besides providing one with different decorations, did actually give one a different atmosphere. Later, in Athens, I spent a more modest but somewhat similar evening, and there each place we visited had its own clientele and its own definable character. It was during about the third halt in the pilgrimage I have just described that I began to recognize the same faces crossing and re-crossing our path. There seemed to be about a hundred or so people in Montmartre that night, all doing the same round as ourselves. In each cabaret the professional dancers employed by the house varied (in identity, but very little in type), but the clientele was substantially the same. During an evening's amusement in London one suffers almost every kind of boredom, but not that. The system by which London night clubs really are clubs, to which one is introduced and elected, tends to preserve a certain integrity of atmosphere. People do not want to multiply subscriptions indefinitely, and for the most part confine themselves to membership of one cocktail and one dancing club. The system of guest fees encourages them to choose the same clubs as the majority of their friends, so that each set has what practically amounts to an established headquarters and rendezvous. Another advantage which the club system gives to London over Montmartre, is that when one's subscription is paid one has the right of membership to eat and drink what one likes.

Le champagne obligatoire of Montmartre is no doubt an economic necessity to the proprietors, but it is an exasperating imposition to those who honestly prefer beer or other wines; moreover, the champagne is notoriously of the most dubious sort.

Two incidents of this visit to Paris live vividly in my memory, and comfort me during sleepless nights, plays, gossip about people I do not know, good advice from my agent about the 'sort of stuff you can put across editors', and the hundred and one other occurrences of daily life when one has to look to oneself for support and consolation.

One of these was the spectacle of a man in the Place Beauveau, who had met with an accident which must, I think, be unique. He was a man of middle age and, to judge by his bowler hat and frock coat, of the official class, and his umbrella had caught alight. I do not know how this can have happened. I passed him in a taxi-cab, and saw him in the centre of a small crowd, grasping it still by the handle and holding it at arm's length so that the flames should not scorch him. It was a dry day and the umbrella burnt flamboyantly. I followed the scene as long as I could from the little window in the back of the car, and saw him finally drop the handle and push it, with his foot, into the gutter. It lay there smoking, and the crowd peered at it curiously before moving off. A London crowd would have thought that the best possible joke, but none of the witnesses laughed, and no one to whom I have told this story in England has believed a word of it.

The other incident happened at a night club called *Le Grand Ecart*. To those who relish the flavour of 'Period', there is a rich opportunity for reflection on the change that came over this phrase when the Paris of Toulouse-Lautrec gave place to the Paris of M. Cocteau. Originally it means the 'splits' – that very exacting figure in which the dancer slides her feet farther and farther apart until her body rests on the floor with her legs straight out on either side of her. It was thus that La Goulou and La Mélonite – 'the Maenad of the Decadence' – and all the jolly girls of the Moulin Rouge were accustomed to complete their *pas seul*, with a roguish revelation of thigh between black silk stocking and frilled petticoat, while the late impressionists applauded through a haze of absinthe. It is not so today. It is the name of a night club with little coloured electric bulbs, decorated with coils of rope and plate glass mirrors; on the tables are little illuminated tanks of water, with floating sheets of limp gelatine in imitation of ice. Shady young men in Charvet shirts sit round the bar repairing with powder-puffs and lipstick the ravages of grenadine and *crème de cacao*. I was there one evening in a small party. A beautiful and splendidly dressed Englishwoman – who, as they say, shall be nameless – came to the next table. She was with a very nice-looking, enviable man who turned out later to be a Belgian baron. She knew someone in our party and there was an indistinct series of introductions. She said, 'What did you say that boy's name was?'

They said, 'Evelyn Waugh.'

She said, 'Who is he?'

None of my friends knew. One of them suggested that she thought I was an English writer.

She said, 'I knew it. He is the one person in the world I have been longing to meet.' (You must please bear with this part of the story: it all leads to my humiliation in the end.) 'Please move up so that I can come and sit next to him.'

Then she came and talked to me.

She said, 'I should never have known from your photographs that you were a blond.'

I should not have known how to answer that, but fortunately there was no need as she went straight on. 'Only last week I was reading an article by you in the *Evening Standard*. It was so beautiful that I cut it out and sent it to my mother.'

I said, 'I got ten guineas for it.'

At this moment the Belgian baron asked her to dance. She said, 'No, no. I am drinking in the genius of this wonderful young man.' Then she said to me, 'You know, I am psychic. The moment I came into this room tonight I *knew* that there was a *great personality* here, and I knew that I should find him before the evening was over.'

I suppose that real novelists get used to this kind of thing. It was new to me and very nice. I had only written two very dim books and still regarded myself less as a writer than an out-of-work private schoolmaster.

She said, 'You know, there is only one other great genius in this age. Can you guess his name?'

I suggested Einstein? No . . . Charlie Chaplin? No . . . James Joyce? No . . . Who?

She said, 'Maurice Dekobra. I must give a little party at the Ritz for you to meet him. I should feel I had at least done something to justify my life if I had introduced you two great geniuses of the age. One must do something to justify one's life, don't you think, or don't you?'

Everything went very harmoniously for a time. Then she said something that made me a little suspicious, 'You know, I so love your books that I never travel without taking them all with me. I keep them in a row by my bed.'

'I suppose you aren't by any chance confusing me with my brother Alec? He has written many more books than I.'

'What did you say his name was?'

'Alec.'

'Yes, of course. What's your name, then?'

'Evelyn.'

'But . . . but they said you wrote.'

'Yes, I do a little. You see, I couldn't get any other sort of job.'

Her disappointment was as frank as her friendliness had been. 'Well,' she said, 'how very unfortunate.'

Then she went to dance with her Belgian, and when she sat down she went to her former table. When we parted she said vaguely, 'We're sure to run into one another again.'

I wonder. And I wonder whether she will add this book, and with it this anecdote, to her collection of my brother's works by the side of her bed.

TWO

My next move was to Monte Carlo, where I had arranged to join a ship called the *Stella Polaris*, which was to carry me to Constantinople, for I still adhered to my resolution of reaching Russia through the Black Sea. I had spent a good deal more money in Paris than I had meant to, and had lost a little through minor dishonesties (if one has a careless disposition and mild appearance, one has to add about ten per cent on to all one's expenses in France and twenty in Italy, because it seldom occurs to the inhabitants of these countries with whom the tourist comes into contact to offer the correct change until the incorrect has been refused. It takes some time to overcome the English habit of pocketing change unchecked), so I did not travel in a luxurious train or a luxurious manner. A railway journey is always disagreeable to me, and I would sooner suffer to the full, and enjoy the contrast when I reach a house or a ship, than spend a great deal of money in rendering it very slightly more supportable. Accordingly I booked a *couchette*, which, I am told, is the way Frenchmen always travel. It is a carriage for four, with two berths which open from the wall above the seats. You can lie full length on these, covered with rugs. It is one better than sitting up all night and not much more expensive.

My companions in this carriage were a French business man – a commercial traveller, I should think – and a rather sweet-looking young English couple – presumably, from the endearments of their conversation and marked solicitude for each other's comfort, on their honeymoon, or at any rate recently married. The young man was small and pleasantly dressed and wore a slight, curly moustache; he was reading a particularly good detective story with apparent intelligence. His wife was huddled in a fur coat in the corner, clearly far from well. I was to meet this couple again on my travels, so I may as well at once give them the names by which I later learned to call them; they were Geoffrey and Juliet.

Every quarter of an hour or so they said to each other 'Are you quite sure you're all right, darling?' And replied, 'Perfectly, really I am. Are *you*, my precious?' But Juliet was far from being all right. After we had travelled for about an hour, Geoffrey produced a thermometer and took her temperature. They had some difficulty in reading it and translating the Centigrade degrees into Fahrenheit; when they did succeed, they discovered that it registered 104°. Geoffrey was scared, but not nearly as scared as Juliet. The person who was most scared of all was the French commercial traveller. His eyes narrowed at the sight of the thermometer and he shrank back in his corner as though he could ward off infection with his copy of *Le Journal*; an epidemic of 'flu was raging at this time in London and Paris, and I must admit that I, too, felt profound repugnance towards this unfortunate young couple. I began to visualize myself stranded alone in a Riviera nursing-home. Accordingly, when I found myself in conversation with Geoffrey a little later, I gave him what was, apart from my own interest, the perfectly sound advice to move Juliet into a *wagon-lit* for the night. He went down the corridor to look for the *conducteur*. Juliet and the Frenchman and I sat in our corners in an atmosphere of very intense fear and hostility. After a long time Geoffrey came back; he had endured the series of insults to which one is always subjected in a French railway train and secured a transfer. There was only one bed vacant, and it was in a double compartment divided only by a curtain. Geoffrey said that the other occupant was a man, but that he had three books of devotion ranged on the shelf by his pillow, so that he was undoubtedly wholly respectable. So he put Juliet to bed, and spent most of the evening sitting with her in the sleeper.

I met him again in the restaurant car, where we ate the very bad dinner opposite each other at the same table. He had some rather dim job in London; Juliet had been ill and a sister of hers was paying their expenses on a Mediterranean pleasure cruise. They were booked for the *Stella Polaris*; it was the first time he had been farther abroad than Florence; now Juliet had got 'flu; he was very despondent and I attempted to cheer him with cognac; I told him that I, too, was going in the *Stella Polaris* on my way to Russia; he was suitably impressed by my destination.

We returned to our *couchette*, where the Frenchman was putting on four or five brightly coloured woollen jerseys. preparatory to turning in for the night.

How that man snored and grunted!

I slept very little, and when I did was bored by the most prosaic kind of dreams; when daylight came through the edges of the blinds I went out into the corridor. We had travelled through a storm during the night and the windows were completely obscured by frozen snow. A very young priest, who cannot long have left his seminary, was standing in the corridor, steadying himself against the window bars. His chin was blue and his face very pale; he dabbed his nose with a handkerchief.

An hour later, while Geoffrey and I were drinking coffee in the restaurant car, I heard a very sad story about this priest. He was the other occupant of Juliet's *wagon-lit*. He had dined with the late service and returned to his carriage to find Juliet just getting into bed. He had stood in the doorway for one half-minute, his eyes wide with shock. Juliet had made things worse by giving him a feverish smile of welcome. Then, without a word, he fled. He had spent the whole night standing in the corridor, and the night air seemed to have been effective in purging him of any worldly thoughts that the encounter provoked.

The train was an hour or so late owing to the snow, but was very fortunate compared with other trains of that week; the Blue Train next day was held up for nearly six hours, and the Simplon-Orient for several days.

I parted from Geoffrey and Juliet at Monaco. They were going on to Monte Carlo, but I had decided to get out at Monaco because, I was told, the hotels were cheaper, and it would be more convenient for boarding the *Stella Polaris*, though I had inadvertently registered my luggage to Monte Carlo, from where I had it rescued later in the day.

The station at Monaco is very small and unpretending. The only porter I could find belonged to an hotel with a fairly reputable sounding name. He took my suitcase and led me through the snow, down the hill to his hotel. It was a miserable-looking *pension* in a side street. There was a small lounge full of basket chairs in which elderly Englishwomen sat sewing. I asked the porter whether there was not a better hotel at Monaco. Why, yes, he said, all the hotels in Monaco were better than this one. So he picked up my suitcase again and we went out into the snow, pursued by a manageress, and soon reached a large hotel facing the harbour. I do not advise anyone to stay at this hotel, which is neither cheap, smart, quiet, nor comfortable, and the only meal I ate there was the sort of food one has on a railway train. However, as I was out all day, I spent four nights there without any acute dissatisfaction. I learned later that I should have gone to the Monégasque.

After luncheon the snow stopped, and the afternoon turned out intensely cold but bright and clear. I took a tram up the hill to Monte Carlo. The sound of firing came from the bastion below the promenade where '*Tir aux Pigeons*' was advertised. Feeling that if I intended to write a book it was my duty to see all the sights conscientiously (this feeling quickly wore off), I paid a few francs and descended in a gilt lift to the terrace. It was terribly cold. Some kind of match was in progress; the competitors were for the most part South Americans with papal titles. They made very interesting gestures with their elbows as they waited for the little cages to collapse and release the game; they also had interesting gestures of vexation and apology when they missed. But this was rare. The standard of marksmanship was high, and while I was there only three birds, fluttering erratically with plucked tail and wings, escaped the guns, to fall to the little boys below, who wait for them on the beach or in rowing-boats and pull them to pieces with their fingers. Often when the cages fell open the birds would sit dazed among the débris, until they were disturbed with a bowl; then they would rise clumsily and be brought down, usually by the first barrel, when they were about ten feet from the ground. On the balcony above the terrace sat one of the Casino pigeons, privileged and robust, watching the destruction without apparent emotion. The sport seemed unattractive, lacking, as it does, even the artificial spontaneity or artificial utility of English and Scottish shooting parties. The only convincing recommendation which I heard of it came from one of the visitors at the Bristol who remarked that it was not cricket; but even that is only very negative praise.

On the way back down the hill I stopped at the Sporting Club and became a temporary member, and it was here that I learned the solution of a minor problem which had often vexed me. I was always reading in my newspapers about 'clubmen', and it made me wonder who this mysterious race were and if I had ever seen one. Clearly they were rapidly becoming extinct, because, though the papers were full of their deaths, I never read of their births or appointments. I felt it was sad to live in this age and not to see them. One day I should read of the death of the last clubman and should know it was too late. I wondered how many clubs one had to belong to before one could be described as a clubman, or whether it was enough merely to sleep and eat one's meals at a club. The problem presented itself in an acute form when I applied to the secretary of the Sporting Club for temporary membership. He was a gracious and elegant young man, and he said it would be a delight and honour for me to join his club. He began to fill in my *dossier*. Name? Address? Nationality? Profession? Then he sat with the point of his fountain pen poised over the space marked 'Club'. I said that I did not belong to a club in London. He looked disappointed and embarrassed. Surely, he said, I must belong to the Authors' Club. I tried to explain the paradox of English social organization by which it is possible to write books and yet not be a member of the Authors' Club. He clearly did not understand. There were in his mind only two possible explanations; either I was a crook trying to pass myself off as an author, or else I was a renegade and discredited author, an outcast from his fellows, a plagiarist and infringer of copyrights, an illiterate, misleading, and mischievous author, one, no doubt, whose books were bound in plain wrappers and might not be sent through the post. He was very sorry, the secretary said, but only clubmen were eligible for the Sporting Club. The Sporting Club was affiliated to all the leading clubs of Europe and America. The idea of this gay little cocktail-bar-*cum*-gambling-den being in affiliation with, say, the National Liberal Club seemed to me noteworthy. Then, as I turned to go, the vision which this conversation had called up of red leather chairs and old men asleep behind periodicals reminded me of an episode in my past.

'I am a life member of the Oxford Union,' I said. 'No doubt you are affiliated with that society?'

'Why, certainly,' said the secretary. All his good nature returned to him. He made out a little card of membership for me and bowed me to the door.

And the moral of this story is that we are, one and all, clubmen, without our knowledge, and it only comes out when we die.

And the discovery of this fact shows how travel broadens the mind.

That night I dined at the Sporting Club. The dinner was delicious and less expensive than the three or four leading restaurants. I saw, but did not dare to speak to, Joseph, who is one of the famous servants of Europe; he lends money to famous beauties and knows the secrets of the *noblesse industrielle*. After dinner I played roulette and won a hundred francs or so. I went up with them to the Casino, which, by comparison, seemed very shabby. The cinema producer's version of the *salles privées*, with jewelled courtesans and ribboned grand-dukes, is a thing of the past. Nowadays, in the evening, these famous rooms look like Paddington Station in the first weeks of August. There are rows of very dowdy spinsters playing the minimum stake methodically upon the even chance; young men in tweeds who look like, and probably are, accountants on their holiday; a few avaricious retired soldiers, and numerous ugly Germans. I admired the dexterity of the croupiers, particularly those who deal out cards with flat wooden batons. I went back into the other rooms called 'The Kitchen', and played for a little. No one tried to filch my winnings. I, on the other hand, absent-mindedly collected a large pile of valuable square counters belonging to a governess opposite; I hastily restored them, but it was clear from the things she said very audibly under her breath that she had little faith in my apologies. I lost my hundred francs and another hundred and then went back to bed.

In spite of the frost, which showed no sign of breaking, I enjoyed the next three days very well. Once I went up to the palace gardens and visited the aquarium, which is less like a cinema than the one in London, and more like a fish-shop. On another day I took the funicular railway to La Turbie and walked through deep snow to Eze for luncheon. There were two rival restaurants immediately facing each other. I asked advice from an inhabitant as to which was the better, but he said that that was a matter I must decide for myself. This seemed a foolish answer, as there was no way in which I could judge except by having two preliminary luncheons and then a third in the house of my choice, so I did not try to decide but took the one on the left without bothering any more about it, and was rewarded by a perfectly adequate meal and half a bottle of fizzing wine called Royal Provence, which I learned to like some years ago in Tarascon. Most of my meals I had in small restaurants in Monaco and Monte Carlo and Beausoleil. There was a delightful one on the quay, called Stallé's, which was not quite as cheap as it looked, and another on the harbour front, called Marina, where dinner cost only 10 francs and the landlord was anxious to please; another I went to in Monte Carlo was called Giardino's. The food there was good, and it had a small garden with a roof of trellis and vines which I learned to enjoy when I returned later in the summer, but there was a rather self-conscious clientele, many of them from the Russian ballet, and the whole place reminded me too closely of Soho.

Great excitement prevailed during my last day as a result of the visit of three destroyers; two of them were Italian and one British, the *Montrose*. The Italians arrived in the early morning and woke up the principality by firing salutes. The *Montrose* adhered more rigidly to etiquette and caused offence to some of the Monégasques by her unadvertised approach. The three ships lay alongside the quay, and the crowds never tired of comparing them. There was very little doubt about the superior smartness of the *Montrose*, but the salvo of guns had put public opinion warmly on the side of the Italians, and they collected by far the larger audience; incidentally, there always seemed to be more going on in them, and the uniform of their chief officer – I do not know what his rank can have been – outdid in grandeur even the Monégasque sergeants of police. I saw Geoffrey once for a few minutes in the Casino. He was very worried about Juliet, but her sister had cabled more money and she now had an attendant doctor and nurse trying to get her fit to travel in the *Stella*.

A thing which excited my particular admiration was the way in which the Casino authorities dealt with the snow. There was a heavy fall every night I was there, sometimes continuing nearly until midday, but always, within an hour of it stopping, every trace had disappeared. The moment that the last flake had fallen there appeared an army of busy little men in blue overalls armed with brooms and hoses and barrows; they sluiced and scraped the pavements and brushed up the lawns; they climbed up the trees with ladders and shook down the snow from the branches; the flower beds had been overlaid with wire frames, straw, and green baize counterpanes; these were whipped off, revealing brightly flowering plants which were replaced, the moment they withered in the frost, by fresh supplies warm from the hot-houses. Moreover, there was no nonsense about merely tidying the unseemly deposit out of the way; one did not come upon those dirty drifts and banks of snow which survive in odd corners of other places weeks after the thaw. The snow was put into barrows and packed into hampers and taken right away, across the frontier perhaps, or into the sea, but certainly well beyond the imperium of the Casino.

This triumph of industry and order over the elements seems to me typical of Monte Carlo. Nothing could be more supremely artificial, except possibly the india rubber bathing beach which they had just decided to instal, but there is a consistency and temperance and efficacy about the artificiality of Monte Carlo which Paris so painfully lacks. The immense wealth of the Casino, derived wholly and directly from man's refusal to accept the conclusion of mathematical proof; the absurd political position of the state; the newness and neatness of its buildings; the absolute denial of poverty and suffering in this place, where sickness is represented by fashionable invalids and industry by hotel servants, and the peasantry in traditional costume come into town to witness in free seats at the theatre ballets of *Le pas d'acier* and *Mercure*; all these things make up a principality which is just as real as a pavilion at an International Exhibition. It might, indeed, actually be some such pavilion in an exposition arranged in time instead of in space – the Palace of Habitable Europe in the early twentieth century; it seems to me to bear just that relation to our own lives today which Mr Belloc's idea of medieval Christendom, or the sixth form masters' Greek city state, bear to the actual lives of the Greeks at the time of Pericles, or the Christians in the time of St Thomas Aquinas.

THREE

The arrival of the *Stella Polaris* caused every bit as much excitement in Monaco as the three destroyers had done. She came in late in the evening, having encountered some very heavy weather on her way from Barcelona. I saw her lights across the harbour and heard her band faintly playing dance music, but it was not until next morning that I went to look closely at her. She was certainly a very pretty ship, standing rather high in the water, with the tall, pointed prow of a sailing yacht, white all over except for her single yellow funnel, and almost ostentatiously clean; a magnificent Scandinavian sea-man stood at the foot of the gangway, and I could see above him on the main deck the officer of the watch saying goodbye to two or three of the passengers. So far I was agreeably impressed, but I reserved judgement, for she has the reputation of being what is called 'the last word' in luxury design, and I am constitutionally sceptical of this kind of reputation.

During that day I had some opportunity of observing my future fellow passengers, for they mostly arrived early or spent the night before embarkation at the Bristol. Vast quantities of luggage appeared in the vestibule bearing the blue and white labels of the *Stella*; some of this belonged to those who had been on the preceding cruise and were on their way home; these fraternized in the lounge and the cocktail bar with the prospective passengers, and I heard on all sides comparisons of the rigours of the storm as it had been felt in the Mediterranean and the Blue Train. I saw them in the restaurants and the Casino and driving out on the Corniche in hired motor cars – clearly diverse in origin and experience, but imbued, nevertheless, with a certain recognizable conformity of interests which makes them a necessary part of the study of any conscientious analyst of modern social conditions, for they are a type selected and developed by a series of conditions which are wholly peculiar to the present age, and must form part of our 'period' as surely as gossip-writers or psycho-analysts.

I do not really know how genuine or valuable this sense of period is. It is a product of the English public school and University education; it is, in fact, almost its only product which cannot be acquired far better and far more cheaply elsewhere. Cultured foreigners are lacking in it, and so are those admirably informed Englishmen whose education has been at secondary schools, technical colleges, and the modern Universities, or at the Royal Naval Colleges of Dartmouth and Greenwich. I am inclined to think that it is practically valueless. It consists of a vague knowledge of History, Literature, and Art, an amateurish interest in architecture and costume, of social, religious, and political institutions, of drama, of the biographies of the chief characters of each century, of a few memorable anecdotes and jokes, scraps of diaries and correspondence and family history. All these snacks and titbits of scholarship become fused together into a more or less homogeneous and consistent whole, so that the cultured Englishman has a sense of the past, in a continuous series of clear and pretty *tableaux vivants*. This Sense of the Past lies at the back of most intelligent conversation and of the more respectable and worse-paid *genre* of weekly journalism. It also colours our outlook on our own age. We wonder what will be the picture of ourselves in the minds of our descendants; we try to catch the flavour of the period; how will this absurd little jumble of antagonizing forces, of negro rhythm and psycho-analysis, of mechanical invention and decaying industry, of infinitely expanding means of communication and an infinitely receding substance of the communicable, of liberty and inertia, how will this ever cool down and crystallize out? How shall we look in the fancy-dress parties and charity pageants of 2030? So we go through our lives generalizing and analysing, and that, anyway, gives us an impersonal and rather comforting attitude towards them.

Pleasure cruising is a development of the last twenty years. Before that only the very rich, who owned their own yachts, could afford this leisurely pottering from port to port. It is a new sort of travel and it has produced a new sort of traveller, who is without any doubt, a considerable contributor to our period.

Our sense of the past informs us of two kinds of Englishmen abroad

33

in the last century. First there is the survivor of the grand tour; he is invariably male; a young man fresh from the University, well born and wealthy, travelling usually in his own coach, with his own servants; he may have friends with him, or a tutor; he always has a pair of pistols and a great many letters of introduction; a courier has ridden before him to prepare his rooms; he dines at the British embassies and legations and is presented at foreign courts; he admires the Italian marbles, the Opera; the gardens and parks seem to him in no way superior to his own home; he keeps a journal; he has rather adventurous love affairs; perhaps he fights a duel; he goes through France, Italy, Austria, and Germany in this way, dancing, observing, commenting; then he returns after a year or eighteen months with trunks full of presents for his sisters and cousins, and perhaps some pieces of sculpture to dispose about the house, or an antique bronze or some engravings; he is fully equipped for the duties of legislation, and does not, except in his memory, repeat the experience.

But by about 1860 middle-class prosperity and mechanical transport had produced a new type; the Jones, Brown, and Robinson of the picture books, the Paterfamilias of Punch. Paterfamilias, as a rule, travels with his wife and without his children; often there are other adult members of his family with him – a sister or a brother-in-law; he wears a heavy tweed overcoat and a tweed cap with ear flaps in winter; in summer he gets very hot; he has lived all his life in England and has worked very hard and done well; he is over 'on the Continent' for three weeks or a month; he is very jealous of his country's prestige, but he thinks it is better preserved by a slightly blustering manner with hotel proprietors and a refusal to be 'done' than by his predecessor's scrupulous observance of etiquette; he is very suspicious of foreigners, chiefly on the grounds that they do not have baths, disguise their food with odd sauces, are oppressed by their rulers and priests, are dishonest, immoral, and dangerous, and talk a language no one can make head or tail of; he is made to ride upon a donkey far too small for him and suffer other similar indignities; the question of cigar smoke in railway carriages is with him one of particular cogency; with his arrival begins the ignoble trade of manufacturing special trinkets for tourists, horrible paper-weights of local wood or stone, ornaments of odious design, or bits of cheap jewellery for him to take back as souvenirs. The noble products of his age are Baedeker's guide books and Cook's travel agency. Hard on his heels comes the travelling spinster; astute in tracking the English Protestant chaplain; expert in the brewing of bedroom tea; she has arrowroot and biscuits in her Gladstone bag and a warm wrap to put on at sundown; inadequate sanitation is wedded in her mind with the superstitions of Popery. A new stage has been marked. English people have discovered that it is quite cheap to live abroad.

At the beginning of this century Mr Belloc invented a new traveller; again a male type, though it is disastrously aped by emancipated women. 'All the world is my oyster,' said Mr Belloc, 'since men made railways and gave me leave to keep off them.' The pilgrim on the path to Rome wears very shabby clothes, and he carries a very big walking stick. In the haversack on his back he carries a map and garlic sausage, a piece of bread, a sketch book, and a litre of wine. As he goes, he sings songs in dog Latin; he knows the exaltation of rising before daybreak and being overtaken by dawn many miles from where he slept; he talks with poor people in wayside inns and sees in their diverse types the structure and unity of the Roman Empire; he has some knowledge of strategy and military history; he can distinguish geographical features from scenery; he has an inclination towards physical prowess and sharp endurances; he maintains a firm reticence upon the subject of sex.

That was in the days when it was an unusual experience to have marched with an army; since then there has been the war.

There has also been the motor car. Tourist traffic is no longer confined to the railways. There are very few roads in Europe now where one can walk without a furtive circumspection; one may sing away for a mile or so, then there is a roar at one's heels and one is forced to leap for the gutter in a cloud of dust. The pilgrim has become the pedestrian. But to a certain extent the influence of the *Path to Rome* still determines the travel experiences of a great number of intelligent Englishmen. There is a new type of traveller which is represented by nearly all the young men and women who manage to get paid to write travel books. One comes into frequent and agreeable contact with him in all parts of the world; his book, if finished, is nearly always worth reading. It is his duty, he feels, to the publisher who has advanced him his expenses, to have as many outrageous experiences as he can. He holds the defensible, but not incontrovertible, opinion that poor and rather disreputable people are more amusing and representative of national spirit than rich people. Partly for this reason and partly because publishers are, by nature, unwilling to become purely charitable, he travels and lives cheaply and invariably runs out of money. But he finds a peculiar relish in discomfort. Bed bugs, frightful food, inefficient ships and trains, hostile customs, police and passport officers, consuls who will not cash cheques, excesses of heat and cold, night club champagne, and even imprisonment are his peculiar delights. I have done a certain amount of this kind of travelling, and the memory of it is wholly agreeable. With the real travel-snobs I have shuddered at the mention of pleasure cruises or circular tours or personally conducted parties, of professional guides and hotels under English management. Every Englishman abroad, until it is proved to the contrary, likes to consider himself a traveller and not a tourist. As I watched my luggage being lifted on to the *Stella* I knew that it was no use keeping up the pretence any longer. My fellow passengers and I were tourists, without any compromise or extenuation; but we were tourists – and this brings us back to our original argument – of a new kind.

The word 'tourist' seems naturally to suggest haste and compulsion. One thinks of those pitiable droves of Middle West school teachers whom one encounters suddenly at street corners and in public buildings, baffled, breathless, their heads singing with unfamiliar names, their bodies strained and bruised from scrambling in and out of motor charabancs, up and down staircases, and from trailing disconsolately through miles of gallery and museum at the heels of a facetious and contemptuous guide. How their eyes haunt us long after they have passed on to the next phase of their itinerary – haggard and uncomprehending eyes, mildly resentful, like those of animals in pain, eloquent of that world-weariness we all feel at the dead weight of European culture. Must they go on to the very end? Are there still more cathedrals, more beauty spots, more sites of historical events, more works of art? Is there no remission in this pitiless rite? Must reverence still be done to the past? As each peak of their climb is laboriously scaled, each monument on the schedule ticked off as seen, the horizon recedes farther before them and the whole landscape bristles with inescapable beauties. And as one sits at one's café table, playing listlessly with sketch book and apéritif, and sees them stumble by, one sheds not wholly derisive tears for these poor scraps of humanity thus trapped and mangled in the machinery of uplift.

There is nothing of this kind about pleasure cruising; indeed, the qualities which struck me most about this system of travel were its outstanding comfort and leisure. The first day out of Monaco we spent at sea, arriving at Naples early the next morning. As I walked round the decks and lounge with Geoffrey – he had got Juliet on board, but she was confined to her cabin with acute neuralgia – and studied our fellow passengers and the way in which they passed their day, we realized how admirably it all fitted into place and filled a need in modern life. Ships can be very dirty and uncomfortable – I once travelled second class on a Greek steamer from Patras to Brindisi – but even the worst kind of ship has some advantages over the best kind of hotel. The servants are almost always better, probably because they bear a more direct personal responsibility for your comfort; also one escapes that haphazard and disorganized avarice which is a characteristic of hotel life; a ship is not itself a money-making thing. You have bought your ticket at the office on shore and paid them the money. The ship's business is to carry you where you want to go and to make you as comfortable as they can on the journey; they do not count your baths and your cups of tea; there are not regiments of uniformed little boys, spinning swing doors and expecting tips. There is an integrity and decency about a ship which one rarely finds on land except in very old-fashioned and expensive hotels. As far as I can see, a really up-to-date ship has every advantage over an hotel except stability and fresh meat. By any standard the comfort of the *Stella* was quite remarkable. She is a Norwegian owned six-thousand-ton motor yacht, carrying, when full, about two hundred passengers. As one would expect from her origin, she exhibited a Nordic and almost glacial cleanliness. I have never seen anything outside a hospital so much scrubbed and polished. She carried an English doctor and nurse; otherwise the officers and crew, hairdresser, photographer, and other miscellaneous officials were all Norwegian. The stewards came of that cosmopolitan and polyglot race, Norwegian, Swiss, British, Italian, which supply the servants of the world. They maintained a Jeeves-like standard of courtesy and efficiency which was a particular delight to the English passengers, many of whom had been driven abroad by the problem of servants in their own homes. The passengers, too, were of all nationalities, but British stongly predominated, and English was the official language of the ship. The officers seemed to speak all languages with equal ease; several of them had first gone to sea in windjammers; sitting out between dances after dinner, while the ship ran on smoothly at fifteen knots into the warm darkness, they used to tell hair-raising stories of their early days, of typhoons and calms and privations; I think that when they were getting a little bored by their sheltered lives they found these reminiscences consoling.

My cabin was large and furnished like a bedroom; Juliet and Geoffrey were on the deck above me and, thanks to Juliet's sister, occupied a suite of great luxury, with a satinwood panelled sitting-room and their own bathroom. There were four of these in the ship, besides about a dozen state-rooms with private bathrooms. The smoking-room, lounge, and writing-rooms were much like those to be found in any modern ship. The decks were exceptionally broad and there was a very comfortable deck bar sheltered on three sides from the wind. The dining-room had the advantage over many ships that it could seat all the passengers at once, so that meals did not have to be arranged in two services. These, allowing for the limitations of cold storage, were admirable, and almost continuous in succession. It seems to be of the tenets of catering on board ship that passengers need nutrition every two and a half hours. On shore the average civilized man, I suppose, confines himself to two or at the most three meals a day. On the *Stella* everybody seemed to eat all the time. They had barely finished breakfast – which included on its menu, besides all the dishes usually associated with that meal, such solid fare as goulash and steak and onions – before tureens of clear soup appeared. Luncheon was at one o'clock and was chiefly remarkable for the cold buffet which was laden with every kind of Scandinavian delicatessen, smoked salmon, smoked eels, venison, liver pies, cold game and meat and fish, sausage, various sorts of salad, eggs in sauces, cold asparagus, in almost disconcerting profusion. At four there was tea, at seven a long dinner, and at ten dishes of sandwiches, not of the English railway-station kind, but little rounds of bread covered with caviare and *foie gras* with eggs and anchovies. Drinks and tobacco were sold, of course, duty free, and were correspondingly cheap. There were some interesting Scandinavian spirits, drunk as apéritifs, which made me feel rather sick.

Besides these purely fleshly comforts, there was the great satisfaction of not having to fuss about anything. For the real travel-snob, recurrent clashes with authority at customs houses and police stations are half the fun of travelling. To stand for hours in a draughty shed while a Balkan peasant, dressed as a German staff officer, holds one's passport upside down and catechizes one in intolerable French about the Christian names of one's grandparents, to lose one's luggage and one's train, to be blackmailed by adolescent fascists and pummelled under the arms by plague inspectors, are experiences to be welcomed and recorded. But for the simpler sort of traveller there is more comfort in handing his passport to the purser on the first evening of the cruise in the confidence that he will be able to walk down the gangway and saunter off into any town he comes to without molestation or delay. Moreover, nobody, however hard boiled, can really enjoy the incessant packing and unpacking which is entailed in independent travelling, or the nuisance of carrying about with one from hotel to hotel, steamer and *wagon-lit*, an ever increasing collection of dirty clothes. When, as you will read if you persevere so far with this essay, I rejoined the *Stella* later after six weeks on my own, almost the chief satisfaction was to fill my laundry bag, hang up my suits on proper hangers and arrange my brushes and bottles on the dressing-table, and push my trunk under the bed in the knowledge that it would not be wanted again until I reached England.

The passengers for the most part could be divided into two sorts. There were those who were simply travelling on holiday, and there were those who were out to see the world and improve their minds. The first of these were strongly in the majority, and it is for them that pleasure cruising is most aptly suited. They were the elderly people, either singly or in couples, who always avoid English winters. Twenty years ago they would simply have gone to Egypt or Morocco or Southern Europe and spent two months in an hotel. The system of pleasure cruises provides them with greater comfort and a more frequent change of scene at about the same expense. Besides them there were one or two invalids, like Juliet, convalescent after illness or operations. There was also a newly married couple of rather demonstrative disposition. I cannot think of a more extraordinary milieu in which to spend a honeymoon, but these two seemed quite at ease, however shy they made the rest of us feel.

The sight-seers were another matter. For their benefit there was a lecturer who used to give informative addresses in the dining-room after tea. Most of them were girls whose mothers and fathers came under the first heading; between ports they read guide books, played deck games, danced, and fell in love with the officers; many of them kept diaries. A pleasure ship is not the best way to do sight-seeing, but it is by no means a bad one. It depends entirely on what one wants to see. Clearly in a museum or picture gallery the means of conveyance which brought you there are negligible; so far as they affect you at all, the only quality one asks is that they shall not be too tiring. The same applies in an almost equal degree to obviously show places such as Pompeii, but when the object of one's visit is to see places of natural beauty such as the Greek Islands or the Dalmatian Coast, there is a great deal to be said for a less luxurious approach. One of the chief objections is that your time in each place is strictly limited; it is very nice to spend a single day at Gibraltar, but two days at Venice are valueless from the point of view of getting an adequate impression. One cannot curtail or prolong one's stay in accordance with one's sympathies; one can, however, very conveniently reconnoitre for future journeys and decide what places one wishes to visit again at one's leisure.

Another objection is that one's arrival inevitably coincides with a large influx of other visitors, which causes an unnatural outbreak of rapacity among the inhabitants of smaller towns; one is inclined to accept an impression that the whole Mediterranean sea-board is peopled exclusively by beggars and the vendors of souvenirs. Moreover, every place you visit is comparatively crowded; this applies very little to a small ship like the *Stella*, but in the case of the large cruising liners the effect is disastrous to any real appreciation of the country. Places like Venice and Constantinople swallow up this influx without undue indigestion, but the spectacle, which I once saw on a previous visit, of five hundred tourists arriving by car to observe the solitude of a village in the Greek mountains is painful and ludicrous.

Even when you are travelling in a small ship and berthed at a large town, you see a great deal of your fellow passengers on shore; you find them bowing to you in shops and churches and night clubs; they blush with the utmost embarrassment when discovered in less reputable resorts, and wink knowingly at you next morning; they borrow money in Casinos, explaining that they are 'cleaned out' and know that their number is bound to turn up next time. They consult you about tips and stop you in the street to show you things they have bought, and according to your temperament this can be an amusement or a bore. I soon found my fellow passengers and their behaviour in the different places we visited a far more absorbing study than the places themselves.

One particularly interesting type which abounds on cruising ships is the middle-aged widow of comfortable means; their children are safely stored away at trustworthy boarding-schools; their servants are troublesome; they find themselves in control of more money than they have been used to; their eyes stray to the advertisements of shipping companies. And how artistically these are phrased. One of the compensating discoveries one makes when, for any reason, one finds a period of celibacy imposed on one, is that everyone one meets, and many of the commonplace events and occurrences of daily life, become suffused in a delicious way with an air of romance. (I have no doubt that much of the radiant happiness evident in religious communities comes from their source. What a lot of nonsense people will talk about sex repression. In many cases an enforced and unrationalized celibacy does give rise to those morbid conditions which supply material for the jollier passages in the Sunday newspapers. But in healthier psychological organisms, a sublimated sex motive may account for a vast proportion of the beneficial activities of man; copulation is not the only laudable expression of the procreative urge – certainly not copulation in which the procreative motive has been laboriously frustrated. The Christian virtues of charity and chastity have from old time an indissoluble alliance – but all this is hardly to the point.) These widows, then, celibate and susceptible, read the advertisements of steamship companies and travel bureaux and find there just that assembly of phrases – half poetic, just perceptibly aphrodisiac – which can produce at will in the unsophisticated a state of mild unreality and glamour. 'Mystery, History, Leisure, Pleasure', one of them begins. There is no directly defined sexual appeal. That rosy sequence of association, desert moon, pyramids, palms, sphinx, camels, oasis, priest in high minaret chanting the evening prayer, Allah, Hichens, Mrs Sheridan, all delicately point the way to sheik, rape, and harem – but the happily dilatory mind does not follow them to this forbidding conclusion; it sees the direction and admires the view from afar. The actual idea of abduction is wholly repugnant – what would the bridge club and the needlework guild say when she returned? – but the inclination of other ideas towards it gives them a sweet and wholly legitimate attraction.

I do not think these happier travellers are ever disappointed in anything they see. They come back to the ship from each expedition with their eyes glowing; they have been initiated into strange mysteries, and their speech is rich with the words of the travel bureau's advertising manager; their arms are full of purchases. It is quite extraordinary to see what they will buy. At every port some peculiar trinket is peddled, tortoiseshell at Naples, shawls at Venice, vile jewellery at Tangier, tortoises and sponges and olive-wood animals at Corfu, beads and Turkish delight and unseemly picture postcards at Port Said; there is a mysterious trade done at Constantinople in English small change; at Majorca they sell kindergarten basket-work and straw hats, at Algiers binoculars and carpets, at Athens frightful marble statuettes. It is hard to escape without buying something; the widows buy anything they are offered. I suppose it is the housekeeping habit run riot after twenty years of buying electric-light bulbs and tinned apricots and children's winter underwear. They become adept in bargaining and may be seen in the lounge over their evening coffee, lying prodigiously to each other, like the fishermen of comic magazines, comparing prices and passing their acquisitions from hand to hand amid a buzz of admiration and competitive anecdote. I wonder what happens to all this trash. When it reaches England and is finally unpacked in the grey light of some provincial morning, has it lost some of its glamour? Does it look at all like the other bric-à-brac displayed in the fancy goods emporium down the street? Is it distributed among relatives and friends to show that they are not forgotten during the voyage? – or is it treasured, every bit of it, hung upon walls and displayed on occasional tables, a bane to the house-parlourmaid but a continual reminder of those magical evenings under a wider sky, of dance music and the handsome figures of the officers, of temple bells heard across the water, of the inscrutable half light in the bazaars, of Allah, Hichens, and Mrs Sheridan?

There was a series of land excursions organized on board the *Stella* by a patient and very charming Norwegian ex-sea-captain in a little office on the promenade deck, and one of the questions most exhaustively discussed among the passengers was whether these were worth while. I went on one or two of them, and I think that, for those whose main object is to save themselves as much trouble as possible, they are an excellent thing. If one has little experience of travelling and no knowledge of the language of the country one is inevitably cheated a great deal. All the ruffians of every nation seem to concentrate themselves in the tourist traffic. The organized expeditions worked smoothly and punctually; there were always enough cars and enough luncheon; everyone always saw all that had been promised him. I shall describe some of these trips in more detail later. At Naples, where I set out entirely alone with a very little knowledge of Italian, I wished very much that I had joined one of the parties.

We ran into the bay early on Sunday morning, and moored alongside the quay. There was a German-owned tourist ship in the harbour, which we were to see several times during the next few weeks, as she was following practically the same course as ourselves. She was built on much the same lines as the *Stella*, but the officers spoke contemptuously of her seaworthiness. She had capsized, they said, on the day she was launched, and was now ballasted with concrete. She carried a small black aeroplane on her deck, and the passengers paid about five guineas a time to fly over the harbour. At night her name appeared on the boat deck in illuminated letters. She had two bands which played almost incessantly. Her passengers were all middle-aged Germans, unbelievably ugly but dressed with courage and enterprise. One man wore a morning coat, white trousers, and a beret. Everyone in the *Stella* felt great contempt for this vulgar ship.

By the time that we had finished breakfast, all the formalities of passport and quarantine offices were over, and we were free to go on shore when we liked. A number of English ladies went off in a body, carrying prayer-books, in search of the Protestant church. They were outrageously cheated by their cab driver, they complained later, who drove them circuitously and charged them 85 lire. He had also suggested that instead of going to matins they should visit some Pompeian dances. I, too, was persecuted in a precisely similar way. As soon as I landed a small man in a straw hat ran to greet me, with evident cordiality. He had a brown, very cheerful face, and an engaging smile.

'Hullo, yes, you sir. Good morning,' he cried. 'You wanta one nice woman.'

I said, no, not quite as early in the day as that.

'Well then, you wanta see Pompeian dances. Glass house. All-a-girls naked. Vair artistic, vair smutty, vair French.'

I still said no, and he went on to suggest other diversions rarely associated with Sunday morning. In this way we walked the length of the quay as far as the cab rank at the harbour entrance. Here I took a small carriage. The pimp attempted to climb on to the box, but was roughly repulsed by the driver. I told him to drive me to the cathedral, but he took me instead to a house of evil character.

'In there,' said the driver, 'Pompeian dances.'

'No,' I said, 'the cathedral.'

The driver shrugged his shoulders. When we reached the cathedral the fare was 8 lire but the supplement showed 35. I was out of practice in travelling, and after an altercation in which I tried to make all the wrong points, I paid him and went into the cathedral. It was full of worshippers. One of them detached himself from his prayers and came over to where I was standing.

'After the mass. You wanta come see Pompeian dances?'

I shook my head in Protestant aloofness.

'Fine girls?'

I looked away. He shrugged his shoulders, crossed himself, and relapsed into devotion . . .

At dinner that evening at the Captain's table the lady next to me said, 'Oh, Mr Waugh, the custodian at the museum was telling me about some very interesting old Pompeian dances which are still performed, apparently. I couldn't quite follow all he said, but they sounded well worth seeing. I was wondering whether you would care to –'

'I'm terribly sorry,' I said, 'I promised to play bridge with the doctor.'

I did not really enjoy those two days in Naples very much. I was ill at ease all the time, and impelled by a restless sense of obligation to see a great deal more than I intelligently could. As a result I wasted money and saw practically nothing. I should have done far better to have joined one of the conducted tours, but I felt snobbish about this, and also I had an idea that I could do things cheaper by myself. A few hours on shore convinced me of the futility of this view. Baedeker's admirable phrase, 'always extortionate and often abusive', applies perhaps more fitly to the Neapolitans than any other race. When I returned in six weeks' time I had become accustomed to depredation and discourtesy and was able to visit the places I wanted to see in a fairly calm state of mind. During these first wet days at Naples I came very near to that obsession by panic and persecution mania which threatens all inexperienced travellers. I refused the services of official guides with undue curtness, only to fall victim to illiterate touts who trotted at my side in a fog of garlic fumes, explaining the architecture to me in a flood of unintelligible English or attempting to sell me trays full of souvenirs. After the first morning I knew that I was beginning to develop that haunted look I had seen so often in the tourist's eye. I saw very little. I went to the museum and derived some amusement from the spectacle of my fellow passengers furtively applying for tickets to the Gabinetta Pornographica. I stood for some time before what must be one of the most lovely gateways in the world – the triumphal arch of Alphonso of Aragon in the Castel Nuovo, and neither of the two postcard sellers who chattered at my side could quite dispel the delight and exaltation it aroused. I walked for some time about the streets of the old town, where Baedeker commends the 'diverse scenes of popular life'. Small boys with long brown legs were bowling oranges about on the wet lava. The girls, at the orders of the priests, wore thick, dirty stockings. Bedding and washing hung from the windows as soon as the rain stopped; the uneven alleys rose in steps between high tenement houses; the smells were varied and intense but not wholly disagreeable. There were shrines at most of the street corners, honoured with artificial bouquets. Rudimentary trades were being pursued in dark workshops. The women gossiped and scolded at their doors and windows and innumerable balconies. I am not ashamed of enjoying this walk. The detestation of 'quaintness' and 'picturesque bits' which is felt by every decently constituted Englishman, is, after all, a very insular prejudice. It has developed naturally in self-defence against arts and crafts, and the preservation of rural England, and the preservation of ancient monuments, and the transplantation of Tudor cottages, and the collection of pewter and old oak, and the reformed public house, and the Ye Olde Inne and the Kynde Dragone and Ye Cheshire Cheese, Broadway, Stratford-on-Avon, folk dancing, Nativity plays, reformed dress, free love in a cottage, glee singing, the Lyric, Hammersmith, Belloc, Ditchling, Wessex-worship, village signs, local customs, heraldry, madrigals, wassail, regional cookery, Devonshire teas, letters to *The Times* about saving timbered alms-houses from destruction, the preservation of the Welsh language, etc. It is inevitable that English taste, confronted with all these frightful menaces to its integrity, should have adopted an uncompromising attitude to anything the least tainted with ye oldeness.

But in a Latin country no such danger exists in any considerable degree. In England, the craze for cottages and all that goes with them only began as soon as they had ceased to represent a significant part of English life. In Naples no such craze exists because the streets are still in perfect harmony with their inhabitants. With his unfailing discernment Baedeker points firmly and unobtrusively to the essential – 'the diverse scenes of popular life'.

I spent the rest of the day visiting churches, most of which were shut. This was a surprise to me, as I had come to accept the statement so frequently advanced by Roman Catholics in England that their churches are always open for devotion in contrast to the Protestant parish church. I had a list, compiled from Baedeker and Mr Sitwell's *Southern Baroque Art*, of those I wished to see. It was one of the exasperating traits of the Neapolitan cab drivers to nod happily at their directions, drive on an elaborate and I have no doubt circuitous route until they arrived before the façade of the building whose frescoes I wished to see, and then, turning round on the box, smile genially, make the motion of locking a door, and say, '*Chiusa, signore.*' The Church of Sansevero was the only one I succeeded in entering that afternoon, and it amply repaid the trouble we took to find it. The name was new to my driver, but after many inquiries we found a small door in a back street. He left the carriage and went off to fetch the custodian, returning after a great delay with a lovely little barefooted girl who carried a bunch of large keys. We left the slum and stepped into a blaze of extravagant baroque. The little girl pattered round, enumerating the chapels and tombs in a voice of peculiar resonance. The sculpture there is astonishing, particularly Antonio Corradini's 'La Pudicizia' – a gross female figure draped from head to foot in a veil of transparent muslin. I do not see how imitative ingenuity can go further; every line of face and body is clearly visible under the clinging marble drapery; the hands and feet alone are bare, and the change of texture between the marble which represents flesh and the marble which represents flesh closely covered with muslin is observed with a subtlety which defies analysis.

While I was going round, my driver took the opportunity of saying a few prayers. The action seemed slightly out of place in this church, so cold and ill-kept and crowded with all but living marble.

When I had made a fairly thorough tour, the little girl lit a candle and beckoned me to a side door, her face, for the first time, alight with genuine enthusiasm. We went down a few steps and turned a corner. It was completely dark except for her candle, and there was a strong smell of putrefaction. Then she stepped aside and held up the light for me to see the object of our descent. Two figures of death stood upright against the wall in rococo coffins, their arms folded across their chests. They were quite naked and dark brown in colour. They had some teeth and some hair. At first I thought they were statues of more than usual virtuosity. Then I realized that they were exhumed corpses, partially mummified by the aridity of the air, like the corpses at St Michan's in Dublin. There were man and woman. The man's body was slit open, revealing a tangle of dry lungs and digestive organs. The little girl thrust her face into the aperture and inhaled deeply and greedily. She called on me to do the same.

'Smell good,' she said. 'Nice.'

We went up into the church.

47

I asked her about the corpses. 'They are the work of the priest,' she said.

Next day I wasted a great deal of time at the aeroplane station trying unsuccessfully to induce a very amiable Italian, to whom I had an introduction, to give me a free flight to Constantinople. After luncheon I drove to Pozzuoli to see a very boring volcanic eruption. The guide who took me round pretended that he could set the gas alight with a piece of smouldering tow. He was about six feet six in height, and wore an astrakhan collar on his overcoat. He seemed so crestfallen at the obvious failure of his demonstration that I felt impelled to cheer him up with a few words of admiration. But this is the wrong line to take with Italians. You should always belittle their goods and they will respect you. The slightest courtesy renders you contemptible. From the moment my guide thought he had taken me in with his pathetic scientific experiment he became domineering and querulous. (I remember an almost precisely similar incident in the chemistry laboratory at my school.)

On the way back I visited the aquarium. I do not know its value among ichthyologists, but as an 'artistic entertainment' it seemed to me very much inferior to the one in London; it smelt. I had tea at Bertolini's, still alone and still very much depressed. The whole bay of Naples and Vesuvius were blotted out by mist.

We sailed that evening during dinner. I came upon poor Geoffrey disconsolately reading *L'Illustration* in the smoking-room. Juliet's neuralgia was better, but her temperature was still high. She had not eaten any dinner. He seemed to have spent most of the day cabling to her sisters.

We reached Messina early next morning, and almost all the passengers went off in motor cars to Taormina, rejoining the ship late in the afternoon at Catania. Geoffrey and I went on shore, and drove round the town in a little horse carriage, visiting the meagre concrete buildings that are slowly rising to replace the desolation of the great 1908 earthquake. It is astonishing how little has been done and in what a niggardly manner. It is a magnificent site for a town, with its long open bay and background of hills and vineyards. The new commercial and residential streets are devoid of any beauty or dignity. The churches make some half-hearted attempts to attract – particularly San Juliano, where the baptistry in concrete Gothic is clean and tall and well conceived. In the square opposite the cathedral, against the background of corrugated iron and builders' litter, stands, apparently uninjured, the very lovely Renaissance fountain by Montorsoli. Its grace and richness of design and the patina of the marble were all the more moving for the ramshackle squalor of their surroundings. This contrast was still more noticeable in the cathedral. We entered through a builders' yard, heaped with fragments of sculpture. The interior was full of scaffolding, and workmen were trotting about busily on all sides pushing barrows, carrying sacks of cement and steel girders. The huge baroque altar and reredos, covered in some places with sacking, in others by dust and fragments of stone, glowed between the scaffolding, while exquisite shrines of inlaid marbles were being gradually pieced together against the raw concrete walls. We walked about for some time in the twilight of the cathedral, unmolested by guides or custodians, and only a little scared by the occasional cataracts of tools and masonry which fell from the ceiling round our feet. We rejoined the ship and lunched almost alone with the officers, while we cruised down to Catania in calm water. The weather was now very fine. We sat on the boat deck and studied the shore through binoculars. Taormina was clearly visible, and the flow of lava from a recent volcanic eruption. The little train that ran down to Catania seemed to make a great deal more smoke than Etna.

Catania looked dirty and uninviting from the sea. A motor boat came out to meet us full of harbour officials, quarantine officers, passport inspectors, and so on, most of them in very fine uniforms with cloaks and swords and cocked hats. The companion ladder was let down for them, but there was some swell on in the harbour and they found difficulty in boarding. As the boat rose towards the ladder the officials stretched out their hands to the rail and towards the massive Norwegian seaman who was there to assist them. Some succeeded in catching hold, but each time their courage failed them just when the boat was at its highest; instead of stepping firmly from the motor boat, they gave a little hop and then let go. It was not a very exacting feat; all the passengers returning from Taormina accomplished it without mishap, including some very elderly ladies. The Sicilians, however, soon abandoned the attempt, and contented themselves with driving twice round the ship as though to show that they had never really intended coming on board, and then returned to their offices.

Geoffrey and I went ashore for an hour or two. The people seemed urban and miserable, particularly the children, who hung about in little joyless groups at the street corners as only grown men do in happier places. We looked at some interesting baroque churches, one with a concave façade which, I think, is unusual, and saw some fine, murky Caravaggios in the San Nicolo Museum. We were unable to obtain access to the church, however, to see the frescoed roof which Mr Sitwell describes in *Southern Baroque Art*. Geoffrey insisted on investigating a partially excavated Greek theatre of no particular interest.

That evening we headed east with two clear days at sea before reaching Haifa. During these days Juliet developed pneumonia, so I saw little of Geoffrey. Deck games broke out all over the ship. The most exacting of these was called 'deck tennis'; the players stood in pairs on opposite sides of a high net and tossed a rope ring backwards and forwards. Many of the passengers attained an astonishing degree of agility in this occupation. Less fortunate ones rendered themselves ludicrous and unpopular by throwing the rings overboard. Some played with such vigour and persistence that they strained their backs and arms, slipped on the deck and bruised their knees, chafed raw places in the skin of their hands, struck each other in the face, twisted their ankles, and sweated profusely.

There was a milder game which consisted in throwing rope rings over a stump, and a still milder one of propelling wooden quoits along the deck with specially constructed bats, like brooms without bristles. Another was called 'Bull Board'; in this the competitors threw rubber discs on to a black board divided into numbered squares. The gentlest and easiest of all was played by dropping rope rings into a bucket. This was strong favourite among the older passengers, who might be seen furtively practising it whenever they thought the decks were deserted.

A committee was formed, of which I found myself a very helpless member, to organize these sports into a tournament. Each of us was put in charge of one of the games and was responsible for hunting out the competitors and introducing them to their partners and opponents in the heats. In this way everyone on board soon knew everyone else, and was able to verify all his previous speculations about his fellow travellers' origins and inclinations. It was interesting to notice that while the English, on the whole, threw themselves zealously into all the business of organizing, scoring, and refereeing, they were disposed to treat the games themselves with discernible casualness and frivolity. The other nationalities, however, and particularly the Scandinavians, devoted every energy whole-heartedly to the cause of victory.

I should really like, in the manner of *Goodbye to All That*, to fill in some pages at this point with descriptions of my own athletic prowess, but must instead confess that I was defeated in the first round of every one of these games, and was severely rebuked by my partners on two occasions for more than ordinary clumsiness.

We reached Haifa during the night after the second day of sports. It is a small port of undistinguished appearance, built during the end of the last century, on the south shore of the bay of Acre, at the foot of Mount Carmel. I had never heard of it before I went there, though as a matter of fact it is a town of some commercial importance. Lately its name has appeared in the newspapers as the scene of anti-Jewish rioting. It seemed very peaceful on the morning of our arrival; there was no other big shipping in the harbour and a light fall of rain kept most of the inhabitants indoors. They are a mixed and somewhat soft-tempered race, composed of Jews, Armenians, Arabs, Turks, and a great many Germans. A large cement works in the outskirts of the town provides the livelihood of most of them. The houses are square and white without any pretensions to ornament; most of them give the impression of being unfinished. To the south, Mount Carmel appeared through the mist, a bulky headland less than two thousand feet in height, crowned with a monastery. Behind the town the highlands of Galilee were just visible, crest upon crest fading away into the grey sky in successive gradations of obscurity.

Warned by my experience in Naples, I had arranged to go with the organized expedition to Nazareth, Tiberias, and Mount Carmel. Accordingly, I landed immediately after breakfast with the rest of the *Stella* party. The cars were waiting for us on the quayside. I was put into the front seat of a Buick next to the driver, who had a sallow, intellectual face and European clothes. Most of the other drivers wore the *taboosh*; the dragoman in charge of the expedition had huge moustaches that stood out from his face, so that the ends were clearly visible from behind him like the horns of a bison. The few loafers who appeared to stare at us wore the voluminous Turkish trousers which are designed by the faithful to provide accommodation in case of the sudden rebirth of the Prophet. Later we passed several families in Arab costume and a convoy of camels. I had always associated them before with sand and sun and date palms. They seemed out of place in this landscape, for, except for an occasional clump of cactus by the side of the road, these misty purple hills, this gentle downpour of rain, this plethora of Jews, these drab conifers, might surely have been from some grouse-laden corner of the Scottish highlands. It raised a curious confusion in the mind by this association of Bonny Prince Charlie with the 'glamour of the inscrutable East'.

The driver of our motor car was a restless and unhappy man. He smoked 'Lucky Strike' cigarettes continuously, one after the other. When he lit a new one he took both hands off the wheel; often he did this at corners; he drove very fast and soon outdistanced all the other cars. When we most nearly had accidents he gave a savage laugh. He spoke almost perfect English with an American accent. He said he could never eat or drink when he was out with the car; he smoked instead; last month he had driven a German gentleman to Baghdad and back; he had felt ill after that. He never smiled except at the corners, or when, as we swept through a village, some little child, its mother wailing her alarm, darted in front of us. Then he would stamp on the accelerator and lean forward eagerly in his seat. As the child skipped clear of our wheels, he would give a little whistle of disappointment through his teeth and resume his despondent but polite flow of anecdote. This man had no religious beliefs, he told me, no home, and no nationality. He was an orphan brought up in New York by the Near East Relief Fund; he did not know for certain, but he supposed his parents had been massacred by the Turks. He liked America; there were a lot of rich people there, he said. After the war he had tried to get American citizenship, but they had turned him out. He had some very bitter trouble about some 'papers'; I could not quite understand what. They had sent him to colonize Palestine. He did not like Palestine because there were so few rich people there. He hated the Jews because they were the poorest of all, so he had become a Mohammedan. He was allowed a dozen wives but remained unmarried. Women took up time and money. He wanted to get rich and then spend all his time going from one place to another until he died. Perhaps if he became very rich they would let him become an American citizen. He would not settle in America, but he would like, when he travelled about, to say he was American; then everyone would respect him. He had been to London once; that was a good town, full of rich people. And Paris; that was nice, too, plenty of rich people there. Did he like his present job? What else was there to do in a stinking place like the Holy Land? His immediate ambition was to get a job as steward in a ship; not a stinking little ship, but one full of rich people like the *Stella Polaris*. I liked this man.

We went to Cana of Galilee, where a little girl was offering wine jars for sale. They were the authentic ones used in the miracle. If they were too big she had a smaller size indoors; yes, the small ones were authentic, too. Then we drove on to Tiberias, a small fishing village of cubic houses on the Sea of Galilee. There were the ruins of some kind of fort and a white domed public bath of steaming mineral water. We were led into this bath. In the courtyard a kind of picnic was going on; an Arab family sitting on the ground and eating bread and raisins. It was almost dark in the bath; the naked bathers lay about in the steam undisturbed by our intrusion. We lunched at Nazareth in an hotel managed by Germans, and ate omelettes, rissoles, and pork, and drank an uncommendable wine called Jaffa Gold. During luncheon the rain stopped. We went to visit the holy places. Mary's Well, in the central square of the town, is the most likely of these to be genuine. It is a communal fountain of obvious antiquity and traditional design; the present fabric may not date from the beginning of the Christian era, but there is a strong probability that a well of similar design has always occupied the same spot. The villagers coming to draw water must bear a strong resemblance to those of two thousand years ago, except that, instead of the earthenware ewers depicted by Mr Harold Copping, they now carry petrol tins on their heads. The Church of Annunciation is of modern construction and meagre design, but it is approached through a pretty courtyard containing fragments of early erections. We were shown the site of the Annunciation and Joseph's Workshop; both these were caves. A cheerful Irish monk with a red beard

53

opened the gates for us. He was as sceptical as ourselves about the troglodytic inclinations of the Holy Family. The attitude of my fellow travellers was interesting. This sensible ecclesiastic vexed them. They had expected someone very superstitious and credulous and medieval, whom they would be able to regard with discreet ridicule. As it was, the laugh was all on the side of the Church. It was we who had driven twenty-four miles, and had popped our tribute into the offertory box, and were being gently humoured for our superstition.

Outside the church a brisk trade was done in olive-wood paperweights. Small boys flung themselves at our feet and began cleaning our shoes. A nun sold lace doyleys. An old woman wanted to tell our fortunes. We struggled through these Nazarenes and got back to the cars. Our driver was smoking by himself. The other drivers were ignorant fools, he said. He wasn't going to waste his time talking to them. He looked with derision at the souvenirs we had bought.

'They are of no interest,' he said, 'none whatever. But if you really wished to buy them you should have told me. I could have got them for you at a tenth of the price.' He lunged out with a spanner and rapped an old man over the knuckles who was trying to sell us a fly-whisk. Then we drove on. The hills were covered with asphodel and anemones and cyclamen. We stopped him, and I got out to pick a bunch for Juliet.

'They will all die before you get back to the ship,' said the driver.

We went back to Haifa, and through the town to the Monastery on Mount Carmel. This has little to show of any architectural interest, as it has been subject to successive demolitions and spoliations since its foundation. The British Governor of Acre in the Napoleonic wars carried off all its treasure, and the Turks used it as a hospital in 1915. There are some shocking frescoes representing the history of the order, by one of the present brothers. The cave, however, over which it is built, known as Elijah's Cave, is a spot of peculiar sanctity, being revered alike by Jews, Mohammedans, and Christians. The Carmelites are one of the few important Latin orders in the East, and they observe that peculiar liaison between Christianity and paganism that is such a feature in the Eastern Churches. During one week in the year, the Arabs bring their children to Carmel, and the monks bless them and perform the ceremony of shaving their heads. During this week the whole hillside is turned into an encampment; the Arabs bring presents of oil, incense, and candles. No attempt is made to convert them to Christianity; they go away, as they came, with camels and horses and numerous wives, thoroughly conscientious Mohammedans. (An interesting book might be written on this subject. At Sinai I am told there is a mosque inside the monastery cloister, and the bell for mass is rung daily by the Mohammedan priest.) An English monk, with the diction and tone of voice of an archdeacon, showed us over. There was a picture postcard stall in the cloister kept by a monk who attempted to give me the wrong change.

We left Haifa for Port Said at dinner-time, and ran almost immediately into heavy weather. The battens, called 'fiddles' by the good sailors, were put out on the tables, and the stewards went round the cabins disposing all breakable objects on the floor. There was no dancing that evening. Poor Geoffrey had spent the day with the ship's doctor securing the services of a nurse. They secured a squat young woman of indeterminable nationality, who spoke English of a sort and had had hospital training. She spent the first half-hour scrubbing Juliet and tumbling her from one side of the bed to the other till her temperature rose to formidable heights. Then she scraped her tongue with a nail file. Then she was very sick and retired to her cabin, and poor Geoffrey, who had been up all the night before, shared another night's vigil with the stewardess (whom the nurse addressed as 'sister'). They sent this nurse back by train from Port Said. It was the first time she had been at sea. Despite the fact that she had spent the whole of her voyage prostrate in her cabin, she expressed the utmost delight in her experience and applied to the doctor for a permanent position on board. After she had gone Geoffrey found an odd document in the cabin. It was a sheet of the ship's notepaper. At the very top, above the crest, was a line of very unsteady pencil handwriting. 'Pneuminia (*La Grippe*) is a very prevalent epidemic Disease in the spring it is.'

Many of the passengers left the *Stella* at Haifa and went on to Egypt by way of Damascus and Jerusalem, rejoining her eight days later at Port Said. The others stayed on board for the night and left next morning by train for Cairo and Luxor. Geoffrey, Juliet, and I, and the two other invalids, were left on board after the first day at

Port Said. Everyone on board values this week of inaction in the middle of the cruise. The officers change into mufti and go shopping at Simon Arzt; the sailors and stewards go ashore in jolly batches of six and seven. It is about the only opportunity they have for prolonged land excursions; several of them went up to Cairo for the day. Those who are on duty are employed in renewed prodigies of cleaning, polishing, and painting. We were filled up with fuel and water. The band played on shore in one of the cafés. The Captain gave luncheon-parties to officials and friends. The sun was brilliant and warm without being too hot, and for the first time we were able to sit comfortably on deck without scarves or greatcoats, and watch the continual coming and going of the big ships in the canal basin.

This was a spectacle of inexhaustible variety. Often there would be as many as four or five first-class liners in the harbour at one time, English, French, German, Italian, Dutch; cargo ships of all sizes from all parts of the world; emigrant ships, troop ships, tourist ships. The ferry boat paddled backwards and forwards, taking gangs of black and incredibly ragged workmen to the coal yards on the east side. There were always innumerable little rowing-boats circling round the ship in the hope of picking up a fare, their boatmen keeping up a soft halloing of self-advertisement; there were the coolies trotting up and down the ladders with sacks of coal, chanting in time and apparently quite unhurried by the whacks and smacks of their overseer; there were the dredgers ceaselessly at work, day and night, with a sound like sea lions at feeding-time; there were fast motor launches filled with harbour officials, always dashing from ship to shore, and almost upsetting with their wash the unstable rowing-boats. Beyond all this bustle we could see the low buildings of the town, a few trees, and, standing out from the shore on its own promontory, the domed and arcaded offices of the canal company; next to it, and modestly emulous in design, stands Navy House, from whose balconies the wives of British officers watch with wistful eyes the P. & O. ships bearing their sisters home on leave, while on the terrace below them Tommies in shirt-sleeves dangle baited hooks into the water and wait with indomitable tenacity the rare advent of some wholly uneatable little fish.

The only disturbing element in this happy week was Juliet, who was by this time very seriously ill. The doctor pronounced her unfit for travel, and she was accordingly lowered in a stretcher and taken ashore to the British hospital. I accompanied the procession, which consisted of the ship's doctor, carrying warm brandy and a teaspoon, an officer, Geoffrey, half distracted with anxiety, a dense mob of interested Egyptians, Copts, Arabs, Lascars, and Sudanese, and a squad of ambulance men, two of whom fought the onlookers while the others bundled Juliet – looking distressingly like a corpse – into a motor van. These last men were Greeks, and refused all payment for their services. It was sufficient reward that they were allowed to wear uniform. They must be the only people in the whole of Egypt who have ever done anything for nothing. I met one of them some weeks later marching with a troop of Boy Scouts, and he fell out of the ranks and darted across the road to shake my hand and ask me news of Juliet in French far worse than my own.

It was a melancholy journey to the hospital, and a still more melancholy walk back with Geoffrey. The British hospital lies at the far end of the sea front. We passed a game of football, played enthusiastically upon an uneven waste of sand, by Egyptian youths very completely dressed in green and white jerseys, white shorts, striped stockings, and shiny black football boots. They cried "ip-'ip-'ooray" each time they kicked the ball, and some of them blew whistles; a goat or two wandered amongst them, nosing up morsels of lightly buried refuse.

We stopped on the terrace of the Casino Hotel for a drink, and a conjuror came and did tricks for us with live chickens. These are called 'gully-gully men' because of their chatter. They are the worst possible conjurors but excellent comedians. They squat on the ground, making odd clucking noises in their throats and smiling happily, and proceed with the minimum of deception to pop things in and out of their voluminous sleeves; their final trick is to take a five-piastre piece and drop that up their sleeve, but it is a good entertainment the first two or three times. There was a little Arab girl in the town who had taught herself to imitate them perfectly, only, with a rare instinct for the elimination of inessentials, she used not to bother about the conjuring at all, but would scramble from table to table in the cafés, saying, 'Gully-gully,' and taking a chicken in and out of a little cloth bag. She was every bit as amusing as the grown-ups and made just as much money. On this particular afternoon, however, Geoffrey was not to be consoled so easily, and the performance seemed rather to increase his gloom. We went back to the ship, and I helped him pack up his luggage and move it to his hotel.

Two days later I decided to join him. The news from the Black Sea was discouraging; heavy storms were raging, some of the ports were still icebound, and very few ships were running regularly; everyone I met told me that it would take at least six weeks to get a Soviet visa. What with this and a feeling of genuine compassion towards Geoffrey and Juliet, I gave up all idea of Russia and determined rather on the less ambitious enterprise of compiling the first travel book to deal extensively and seriously with Port Said; accordingly, I settled there for the next month, and this chapter contains a summary of my investigations.

The town is built on a dead flat patch of sand bounded on the north by the Mediterranean Sea, on the east by the Suez Canal, on the south by Lake Menzaleh, and trailing off westward in a series of indeterminate sand dunes to the Nile Delta. It is thus an island joined to the mainland by a strip of sand between Lake Menzaleh, and the Canal, just broad enough for railway-lines and a high road. On its Mediterranean front it is 'making land' yearly at an astonishing speed, and it is on this recently formed northern territory that the European quarter has been built. The principal arterial thoroughfare in the centre of the town, joining the Arab quarter to the harbour, still bears the name Quai du Nord from the time when it formed the extremity of the town. The principal buildings, the Governor's House, the Casino Hotel, the British and Egyptian hospitals, the schools, and the houses of the richest inhabitants were all built before the war upon the new sea front, and already a vast, firm *plage* has crept up between the road and the sea, ripe for further development; this causes some anxiety, particularly to the hotel proprietors, who depend upon ready access to the sea as an important palliation of their other many inadequacies.

The hotel where Geoffrey and I stayed was on the front – a brand new concrete building kept by a retired English officer and his wife. We chose it because it was near the hospital and comparatively cheap; it was recommended by all the British colony in Port Said on the grounds that it was the only place where you could be certain of not meeting any 'gyppies'. The people we did meet were certainly very British but far from gay. Few people stay in Port Said except for some rather dismal reason. There were two genial canal pilots who lived at Bodell's permanently, and there was an admirable young lawyer just down from Cambridge who added immeasurably to our enjoyment; he was spending his holiday from the Temple in investigating the night life of Alexandria, Port Said, and Cairo. As some people can instinctively find the lavatories in a strange house, this young man, arriving at the railway station of any town in any continent, could instantly orientate himself towards its disreputable quarter. But apart from him and the pilots, the other guests at Bodell's were all people on their way through who had been obliged to leave their ships by the illness of wives or children. There was a planter from Kenya with a small daughter and governess; he was returning home for the first time after fourteen years; his wife was lying desperately ill in the hospital. There was a captain in the Tank corps, on his way out to India for the first time, whose wife had developed appendicitis and had been rushed to the operating theatre. There was a soldier's wife taking her children home for the hot season; her youngest son had developed meningitis. I grew to dread the evenings at home, when we all sat round in wicker armchairs dolefully discussing the patients' progress, while the gentle Berber servants, with white gowns and crimson sashes, stole in and out with whiskies and sodas, and Mr Bodell attempted to cheer us up with an ancient gramophone and an unintelligible gambling game played with perforated strips of cardboard.

There are two large hotels in Port Said, the Eastern Exchange and the Casino, whose marked differences in character typify the change which has come over the town in recent years. The Eastern Exchange is the older and less esteemed; it stands at a busy street corner among the shops and cafés and rises above them in tier upon tier of glass-fronted, steel-framed balconies. The bar is very large, and full of rather decayed leather armchairs and steel pillars. A great deal of heavy drinking goes on there, and the whole place has a distinctly dissolute air. The servants are all Sudanese or Berbers in native costume; shop girls from Simon Arzt's store dance there in the evenings; it is unusual to see anyone in evening dress; Egyptian officials give parties there; English commercial agents stay there and jolly groups of officers from the liners; the food is by far the best in the town and the drinks expensive but pure. The bedrooms are for the most part arranged in large, under-furnished suites. There was always a bustle of coming and going, people recognizing old acquaintances, quarrelling with the servants, consulting the blackboard on which were chalked up the times of the departure of ships.

The Casino stands at the corner of the sea front and the harbour, well away from the shops and cafés, among shipping offices, apartment houses, and government buildings, looking out along the breakwater to the Lesseps statue. It is solidly amd pompously built of concrete, and advertises a minute but carefully tended garden at the back. It would like, if it could, to achieve an air of the French Riviera. The servants are mostly Europeans and Greeks in shabby evening suits; the food is poor. On gala nights there is a *boule* table, the proceeds of which go to local charities.

Every Saturday evening there is a dance to which printed invitations are issued, and the European society of Port Said turns up in force, very self-conscious in dinner-jackets and tulle. Balloons, cardboard trumpets, dolls, and artificial noses are distributed. Every consulate had its table and maintains a certain diplomatic reserve. Next to them in social importance come the three British doctors, the two lawyers, the chaplain, the A.S.C. officers and their wives from Navy House, the British head of police, the shipping office and bank managers. Anyone in British service counts higher than anyone in Egyptian service. The nurses from the hospital are eagerly pursued as partners. But the standards of Port Said society, though wide, are rigid. At the Casino one sees the young men at Cook's office who sell railway tickets, but not the young men at Simon Arzt's who sell sun helmets. Egyptians are not excluded but very few of them attend. Sometimes passengers off the liners appear, inclined to gaiety after the dull canal passage. These are welcomed but freely criticized. While I was there a young woman from an outward-bound P. & O. danced without stockings. I daresay she is still being discussed. There was also a young man who put on a *taboosh* and was officially rebuked by a glance from the British consul. Nearly all the gentlemen of Port Said drink a little too much on these Saturday evenings, and may be seen at half-past eleven next morning sitting round in the club with cups of Bovril and Worcester sauce – declaiming ungratefully against the Casino's whisky.

This club is a very important part of Port Said life. All tolerably respectable British male residents are members, and strangers are hospitably enrolled for the period of their visit. Everyone we encountered, Mr Bodell, the doctors at the hospital, the chaplain, the manager of the bank where we cashed our letters of credit, kindly volunteered to introduce us to the club. It occupies the floor above the Anglo-Egyptian Bank, and consists of a billiard-room, writing-room, smoking-room, balcony, and bar. It is furnished with large armchairs and photographs of the Royal Family and of generals and admirals in the last war. The smell of deodorizers predominates until evening, when tobacco smoke takes its place. Bridge, snooker, and poker dice (for drinks) are the chief occupations; *Punch*, the *Illustrated Sporting and Dramatic News*, and the weekly edition of the *Daily Mirror* the chief intellectual interests. Conversation is vigorous and emphatic, though limited in scope. There seemed an abundance of genuine, if undiscriminating, good-fellowship. 'All the trouble in this town is made by the women,' one of the members told me, and, except for some mild intrigues at the time of the committee election, I saw nothing but harmony and concord on all sides.

It seemed to me that the life led by these oversea business men and officials was in every way agreeable and enviable when compared with its counterpart in modern England. There was, of course, no nonsense of tropical romance; no indomitable jungle, no contact with raw nature, no malaria, delirium tremens, or 'mammy-palaver'; no one showed the smallest inclination to 'go native'; no one was eating out his heart for the lights of Piccadilly or yew walks of a manorial garden; they did not play their bridge with greasy cards or read and re-read a year-old newspaper; no one was 'trying to forget'. One must go to other parts of Africa for that. Port Said is highly respectable and almost up to date. They certainly did not read new books, but then they did not read old books either; they had gramophone records of musical plays still running in London; their newspapers were ten days old, but they had their own *Tatler*, an illustrated gazette of English and American society called the *Sphinx*. (Incidentally, it was in this paper that I noticed a device which I recommend to the English illustrated Press. There was a photograph of four pleasant, plain people blinking into the sunlight, reproduced twice in the same issue with different names beneath each.) The routine of the day was leisured, broken by a very long luncheon interval during which the younger people played tennis and their elders dozed; everyone assembled at the club at six o'clock to read the papers and chat. In the evening there were rehearsals for amateur theatricals and a great many dinner-parties. At one of these my hostess, on leaving the dining-room, paused at the door to say, 'Goodbye, darling men, and keep your naughty stories for us.'

The women seemed peculiarly carefree; they live in manageable modern flats and are served by quiet native men-servants, whose response to all orders, however ill-comprehended, is a deferential inclination of the head and a softly spoken 'All right'. No one is troubled by social aspirations because there is no direction in which to aspire; everyone knows everyone else, and there are no marked disparities of income. No one wants particularly to keep a car, as there is nowhere to drive except the French club at Ismailia.

The men live within five minutes' walk of their work, they have none of that feverish bustling in and out of railway trains and omnibuses which embitters middle-class life in London. More than this, they are, almost without exception, the employees of important firms; they act merely as local agents, with strictly limited responsibilities and nicely defined powers, enjoying absolute security of income, and looking forward to regular degrees of promotion and ultimate superannuation and pension. They are thus serenely ignorant of the anxieties that beset the small company director; the yearly struggle to present a plausible balance sheet to the shareholders' meeting; the harassed perusal of the national budget which may, by some new incidence of taxation, close carefully prepared markets and turn a marginal profit into a dead loss. They live in a Utopian socialist state untroubled by the ardours and asperities of private enterprise. I think many of them were conscious of the peculiar felicity of their lives. Certainly, those who had lately been home on leave had returned with a slightly dissatisfied air. England was changing, they said; damned Bolshies everywhere. 'You have to come outside England,' one of them told me, 'to meet the best type of Englishman.'

I saw practically nothing of the French colony, but I imagine that their life is very similar. They have their own club, but I think that most of their social interests centre in Ismailia, a newly built residential town up the canal. The French consul was the only man I ever saw win consistently at *boule* at the Casino. There were a great number of Greeks, but all of a poorer class, artisans, hairdressers, and the keepers of small shops. They have the largest church in a town bristling with ecclesiastical architecture. Except for Simon Arzt and one admirable French confectioner, the shops are uninteresting and mainly in Coptic or Egyptian hands. Simon Arzt's is a magnificent emporium selling almost everything you could hope to find in Harrods at a considerably higher price. It opens for all big ships, no matter at what hour of the night they come in.

One of the curses of Port Said, and, indeed, of the whole of Egypt, is the street hawking. One cannot sit down for a moment at any café without being beset by tiny Arab urchins, mostly with moist opthalmic eyes and nasty skin diseases, who attempt to clean your shoes. Mere verbal refusal has no force to discourage. They squat at your feet crying, 'Clin-büts, clin-büts,' and tapping the backs of their brushes together. The experienced resident then kicks them as hard as he can, and they put out their tongues and go on to the next table; the visitor pretends not to notice, and, taking this as a commission, they then proceed to befoul his socks and trouser-ends with black paste. Nor is it sufficient protection to allow the first comer to do this and be done with him; not only will a queue of little boys wait until he has finished and then begin their importunacy, but the same boy will be back in twenty minutes and attempt to clean them all over again. The nuisance gradually abates as one's reputation as a kicker spreads; after a fortnight Geoffrey and I were known as self-reliant and violent customers and lived unmolested, but when, after three weeks, Juliet was well enough to come out with us, the boot-boys, with laudable discernment, decided that we would not want to show temper before the white lady, and renewed their persecution until the end of our visit. Juliet thought them rather angels.

I suppose that this cleaning of boots is the early training for the more ambitious salesmanship which menaces one's peace of mind in the open air. These elder pests usually stay at home when there is no ship in, but that is a rare remission. They peddle European newspapers, chocolates, cigarettes, bead necklaces, amber and ivory cigarette-holders, cigarette cases of inlaid brass and gun metal, *appliqué* embroidery from debased hieroglyphic designs, and picture postcards of unexampled lewdness which they flourish very embarrassingly under one's eyes. Geoffrey bought a packet and sent them in heavily sealed envelopes to various acquaintances in England, thereby, I believe, rendering both himself and them liable to criminal prosecution. The original plates of the photographs are, I learned later, of some antiquity, having been made for sale at the first International Exhibition at Paris and being brought to Port Said for the celebrations at the opening of the Suez Canal. There have been innumerable imitations since, of course, but it seemed to me that these earlier examples left little room for improvement; and it was interesting to observe that, for all their nudity, they are unmistakably 'dated' by that indefinable air of period which we have already discussed.

Besides these there were the 'gully-gully' men and numberless fortune-tellers; the latter carried with them printed extracts from testimonials purporting to be written by Lord Allenby, Lord Plumer, Lord Lloyd, and other distinguished Englishmen, but their predictions were invariably monotonous and non-committal. Europeans have a superstitious respect for Oriental soothsayers which the town Arabs have been quick to commercialize; all camel-boys regularly offer to tell their customers' fortunes before proceeding to offer other, and often less acceptable, services.

The dragomans who infest the tourist quarter of Cairo are of a very much higher class; they all speak at least one European language tolerably well, have a superficial but fairly extensive knowledge of antiquities, and exhibit great courtesy and social charm. They are richly clothed and live in some degree of comfort, usually with four or five wives. Most of them have small farms in the country where they retire at the close of the tourist season. As there is nothing at all in Port Said which any intelligent tourist could wish to see, there are very few dragomans. I only met one – a fine ingratiating rascal with a great black moustache and gold teeth. He took me to the mosque – a tawdry, modern building, overlaid like a teashop with cheap Oriental decorations – and offered to procure me some hashish. I gave him thirty piastres; he returned with admirably simulated circumspection and slipped a packet into my hand, telling me on no account to open it in the street. I bore this furtively back to Bodell's and opened it in my bedroom with Geoffrey and the Cambridge solicitor. Inside we found a ten-piastre tin of amber cigarettes. The laugh was on me. We made several other attempts to obtain hashish, which is a common commodity in an Arab town, but were always met by expressions of blank incomprehension. Every European is assumed to be a spy until it is proved to the contrary, and we were no doubt known to be on amicable terms with the commissioner of police. The drug trade, however, is one of wide ramifications in Egypt. The hashish crop is grown in French Syria and brought either by rail to Cantara or by sea to Port Said. Every imaginable device is employed to smuggle it through the customs, and apparently pregnant Arab wives are subjected to a rigorous pummelling which often results in the discovery of bales of contraband under their black gowns; once in the country the distribution is apparently undetectable, and all important seizures of stock take place at the frontier. It seems to me that it would be well worth the while of some enterprising European to organize this side of the business. Tourist baggage is submitted to a very cursory scrutiny. All that is necessary would be to assemble a dozen or so Europeans at Damascus with large trunks heavily encrusted with hotel and steamship labels. These could be half filled with hashish and cocaine, concealed in sponge bags, boots and shoes, soap boxes, hollow books, and the many other undutiable articles of luggage that are never examined. The gang would then book a round tour to Cairo with a perfectly genuine and unsuspicious guide from one of the reputable travel agencies. One such convoy would be enough to provide a handsome profit for all concerned. As far as I can see, it could be repeated with judicious changes of personnel for as long as the organizers required.

Another and very much safer way of making a fortune, which I have been commending to all my avaricious friends, is to start a night club in Port Said. At present there is nothing of the kind. Large ships are continually arriving for a stay of two or three hours and disgorging a horde of fairly wealthy passengers. Port Said still retains a reputation for low life, and half of them at least are avid to see it. They come prancing on shore. Gambling? Why, certainly, there is the *boule* table in aid of Christian charities at the Casino. Dancing?

65

This way to the Eastern Exchange Hotel. Drinking? Here is a clean, airy café – Bass, Guinness, Johnny Walker, English spoken. Theatre? Why, yes. The Port Said Amateur Operatic Society are performing *The Mikado*, or else there are three excellent American dramas of mother love at the three cinemas. It is not at all what they have been led to expect. So they go off to the Casino and dance for an hour, buy a few frightful trinkets of embroidery or brass work, and go back disconsolately to their ships. I firmly believe that anyone enterprising enough to give them what they want could become a rich man in one season. There are no licensing laws, and he could follow the economical example, set by the proprietors of the fashionable resorts of London and Paris, of making his own champagne downstairs in the basement. Rents are low, particularly in the old part of the town round the docks, where the houses are wooden, two-storeyed buildings with slightly romantic associations. The 'Eldorado' Cinema with its double tier of matchboard boxes would serve excellently. I should imagine that it had been built for this purpose in Port Said's disreputable days. It is, in construction, almost exactly like those breath-taking dancing saloons in films about the Klondyke gold rush. It would be easy to collect a sufficiently amusing cabaret of Arab *can-can* dancers, snake charmers, and so on. A few outcasts might be imported from the 'Blue Lantern' and ranged round the walls to give the place a nasty look. 'Jungle-wallahs', returning from lonely outposts of commerce, would find it delightfully civilized and up to date, while, at the next table parties of tourists and officials going out for the first time would sit no less entranced at this introduction to the glamour of the East.

It is only since the war, and largely, I understand, owing to the efforts of the present head of police, that Port Said has become so respectable. From the years when it first grew up round the mouth of the canal it became a harbour for all the most thorough-going type of international riff-raff, and its reputation as a sink of iniquity grew with the town's importance. And, as is always the case, the literary myth survives long after the event. While I was at Bodell's he showed me a recently published magazine story about Port Said, describing the 'evil-smelling, green canal winding its way between the narrow alley ways where sin and crime walk unashamed'. Well, the canal could never have wound its way among the alleys, nor, I think, was it ever evil-smelling or green, but from all the older residents told me, it was certainly quite true about sin and crime walking unashamed until the militant cleaning up by Teale Bey. Robbery with violence and murder were common occurrences in the streets, and people were unwilling to venture out after dark even into the European quarter, except in twos and threes. Now it is nearly as safe as Plymouth, and very much safer than Marseilles or Naples. Prostitution, which was one of the most prominent features of the town, has sunk to negligible dimensions. Up to and during the war there were brothels in the chief streets round the harbour and over the leading cafés and shops. Today they are all localized, as in most Oriental towns.

Geoffrey, the Cambridge solicitor, and I spent two or three evenings investigating this night-town, called by the residents 'red lamp district'. It lies at the farthest extremity of the town on the shore of Lake Menzaleh, round the little wharf and goods yard of the Menzaleh canal, separated from the shops and offices and hotels by a mile or so of densely populated Arab streets. It is very difficult to find by day, but at night, even without our solicitor's peculiar gifts, we should have been led there by the taxis full of tipsy sailors and stewards, or grave, purposeful Egyptians, that swept by us in the narrow thoroughfare.

We set out after dinner one evening, rather apprehensively, with a carefully calculated minimum of money, and life-preservers of lead, leather, and whale-bone, with which our solicitor, surprisingly, was able to furnish us, we left watches, rings, and tie-pins on our dressing-tables, and carefully refrained from alarming Juliet with the knowledge of our destination. It was an interesting walk. An absurd tram runs up the Quai du Nord, drawn by a mare and a donkey. We followed this for some way and then struck off to the left through Arab Town. These streets presented a scene of astonishing vivacity and animation. Little traffic goes down them and there is no differentiation of pavement and road in the narrow earthen track; instead, it is overrun with hand-barrows selling, mostly, fruit and confectionery, men and women bargaining and gossiping, innumerable barefooted children, goats, sheep, ducks, hens, and geese. The houses on either side are wooden, with overhanging balconies and flat roofs. On the roofs are ramshackle temporary erections for store-rooms and hen-houses. No one molested us in any way, or, indeed, paid us the smallest attention. It was Ramadan, the prolonged Mohammedan fast during which believers spend the entire day from sunrise to sunset without food or drink of any kind. As a result the night is spent in feverish feasting; nearly everyone carried a little enamelled bowl of a food resembling some kind of milk pudding, into which he dipped between bites of delicious-looking ring-shaped bread. There were men with highly decorated brass urns selling some kind of lemonade; there were women carrying piles of cakes on their heads. As we progressed the houses became more and more tumbledown and the street more narrow. We were on the outskirts of the small Sudanese quarter where a really primitive life is led. Then suddenly we came into a rough, highly lighted square with two or three solid stucco-fronted houses and some waiting taxis. One side was open to the black, shallow waters of the lake, and was fringed with the masts of the little fishing-boats, called, I believe, *makaris*. Two or three girls in bedraggled European evening dress seized hold of us and dragged us to the most highly lighted of the buildings; this had 'Maison Dorée' painted across its front, and the girls cried, 'Gol'-'ouse, gol'-'ouse,' 'Vair good, vair clean.' It did not seem either very good or very clean to me. We sat in a little room full of Oriental decorations and drank some beer with the young ladies. Madame joined us, a handsome Marseillaise in a green silk embroidered frock; she cannot have been more than forty, and was most friendly and amusing. Four or five other young ladies came in, all more or less white; they sat very close together on the divan and drank beer, making laudably little effort to engage our attention. None of them could talk any English, except, 'Cheerioh, Mr American.' I do not know what their nationality was. Jewesses, Armenians, or Greeks, I suppose. They cost 50 piastres each, Madame said. These were all European ladies. The other, neighbouring houses, were full of Arabs – horrible, dirty places, she said. Some of the ladies took off their frocks and did a little dance, singing a song which sounded like ta-ra-ra-boom-ty-ay. There was a jolly-sounding party going on upstairs, with a concertina and glass-breaking, but Madame would not let us go up. Then we paid for our drinks and went out.

Then we went next door to a vastly more plebeian house called

Les Folies Bergères, kept by a gross old Arab woman who talked very little French and no English. She had a licence for eight girls, but I do not think hers was a regular establishment. On our arrival a boy was sent out into the streets, and he brought back half a dozen or so Arab girls, all very stout and ugly and carelessly daubed with powder and paint. They sat on our knees and embarrassed us rather, so we made our escape, promising to fetch some friends and return. There was another large house, called Pension Constantinople, which we surveyed from outside but did not enter. All round were the little alleys where the freelance prostitutes lived. These were one-roomed huts like bathing cabins. The women who were not engaged sat at their open doors sewing industriously, and between stitches looking up and calling for custom; many had their prices chalked on the doorposts – 25 piastres in some cases, but usually less. Inside iron bedsteads were visible, and hanging banners worked with the crests of British regiments. Their trade is only among the poorest class of Arab, but sitting, as they were, silhouetted against the light, many of them suggested an attraction which their more sumptuously housed competitors lacked, something of that now banal mystery which captivated the imaginations of so many writers of the last century to the furtive drabs of the northern city streets.

On our way back we came upon another gaily illuminated building called Maison Chabanais. We went in, and were surprised to encounter Madame and all her young ladies from the Maison Dorée. It was, in fact, her back door. Sometimes, she explained, gentlemen went away unsatisfied, determined to find another house, then as often as not they found the way round to the other side, and the less observant ones never discovered their mistake. She was an enterprising, humorous woman, and several times after this we visited her in the evening for a glass of beer and a chat; as long as we paid for the beer she never bothered us to extend our patronage further.

Arab Town, at any hour of the day or night, was a fascinating place to us, and it was astonishing to discover how ignorant the English colony were about it, and how uninterested. Many of them had never been there at all. Although it was only a few streets away, they were as vague about it as Londoners are about Limehouse. They had an idea that it smelled and crawled with bugs, and that

69

was enough for them, though they showed a tolerance of my interest, remarking that every chap has his own game; I was one of those writing johnnies, so of course I had to nose round a bit collecting local colour; jolly interesting too for a chap who was interested in that sort of thing; they would read about it all in my book when that came out; meanwhile, snooker and whisky-soda for them. But it was not local colour or picturesque bits, or even interest in the habits of life of another race, which drew me there day after day, but the intoxicating sense of vitality and actuality. I do not suppose that this part of Port Said is more interesting than any other Oriental town; indeed, probably much less so, but it was the first I visited and the only one where I stayed for any length of time. Their intensely human joviality and inquisitiveness, their animal-like capacity for curling up and sleeping in the dust, their unembarrassed religious observances, their courtesy to strangers, their uncontrolled fecundity, the dignity of their old men, make an interesting contrast with all the wrangling and resentment of northern slums, lightened by fitful outbursts of hysteria. You cannot walk down a poor street in England without hearing some woman in a rage or some child in tears. I do not remember once hearing either of these things in Port Said.

While we were there, Ramadan came to an end with the feast of Bajiram. All the children were given new clothes – those that could not afford a frock wearing a strip of tinsel or bright ribbon, and paraded the streets on foot or in horse-cabs. The streets of Arab Town were illuminated and hung with flags, and everyone devoted himself to making as much noise as he could. The soldiers fired cannonade after cannonade of artillery; civilians beat drums, blew whistles and trumpets, or merely rattled tin pans together and shouted. This went on for three days.

There was a fair and two circuses. Geoffrey and I and the head of the hospital went to the circus one evening, much to the bewilderment of the club. The hospital nurses were very shocked at our going. 'Think of the poor animals,' they said. '*We* know the way the gyppies treat their animals.' But, unlike European circuses, there were no performing animals.

We were the only Europeans in the tent. The chairs were ranged on rather unstable wooden steps ascending from the ring to a

70

considerable height at the back. Behind the back row were a few heavily curtained boxes for the women; there were very few there; most of the large audience consisted of young men, a few of them in ready-made suits of European pattern, but all wearing the red *taboosh*. A number of small boys were huddled between the front row and the ringside, and a policeman was employing his time in whisking these off the parapet with a cane. The seats seemed all to be the same price; we paid 5 piastres each and chose places near the back. Attendants were going about between the rows selling nuts, mineral waters, coffee, and hubble-bubbles. These were of the simplest pattern, consisting simply of a coconut half full of water, a little tin brazier of tobacco, and a long bamboo mouthpiece. The doctor warned me that if I smoked one of these I was bound to catch some frightful disease; I did so, however, without ill effect. The vendor keeps several alight at a time by sucking at each in turn. We all drank coffee, which was very thick and sweet and gritty.

The show had begun before we arrived, and we found ourselves in the middle of a hugely popular comic turn; two Egyptians in European costume were doing cross-talk. It was, of course, wholly unintelligible to us; now and then they smacked or kicked each other, so I have no doubt it was much the same as an English music-hall turn. After what seemed an unconscionable time the comedians went away amid thunderous applause, and their place was taken by a very pretty little white girl in a ballet dress; she cannot have been more than ten or twelve years old; she danced a Charleston. Later she came round and sold picture postcards of herself. She turned out to be French. To those that enjoy moralizing about such things there is food for reflection in the idea of this African dance, travelling across two continents from slave to gigolo, and gradually moving south again towards the land of its origin.

Then there were some Japanese jugglers, and then an interminable comic turn performance by the whole company. They sang a kind of doleful folk song and then, one at a time, with enormous elaboration of 'business', came in and lay down on the ground; after all the grown-ups were settled the little girl came in and lay down too; finally a tiny child of two or three tottered in and lay down. All this took at least a quarter of an hour. Then they all got up again, still singing, one at a time in the same order, and went out. After that there was an interval, during which everyone left his place and strolled about in the ring as people do at Lord's between the innings. After this a negro of magnificent physique appeared. First he thrust a dozen or so knitting-needles through his cheeks, so that they protruded on either side of his head; he walked about among the audience bristling in this way and thrusting his face into ours with a fixed and rather frightful grin. Then he took some nails and hammered them into his thighs. Then he stripped off everything except a pair of diamanté drawers, and rolled about without apparent discomfort on a board stuck with sharp carving-knives.

It was while he was doing this that a fight began. It raged chiefly round the exit, which was immediately below our seats. The heads of the combatants were on a level with our feet, so that we were in a wholly advantageous position to see everything without serious danger. It was difficult to realize quite what was happening; more and more of the audience joined in. The negro got up from his board of knives, feeling thoroughly neglected and slighted, and began addressing the crowd, slapping his bare chest and calling their attention to the tortures he was suffering for them. The man on my right, a grave Egyptian with a knowledge of English, with whom I had had some conversation, suddenly stood up, and leaning across all three of us struck down with his umbrella a resounding blow on the top of one of the fighting heads; then he sat down again with unruffled gravity and devoted himself to his hubble-bubble.

'What is the fight about?' I asked him.

'Fight?' he said. 'Who has been fighting? I saw no fight.'

'There.' I pointed to the seething riot in the doorway which seemed to threaten the collapse of the entire tent.

'Oh, that!' he said. 'Forgive me, I thought you said "fight". That is only the police.'

And sure enough, when the crowd eventually parted some minutes later, there emerged from its depths two uncontrollably angry police constables whom the onlookers had been attempting to separate. They were ejected at last to settle their quarrel outside; the crowd began sorting out and dusting their fallen fezes; everything became quiet again, and the big negro resumed his self-lacerations in an appreciative calm.

72

Various forms of acrobatics followed in which the little French girl displayed great intrepidity and style. It was in full swing when we left, and apparently continued for hours nightly until the last comer felt he had had his money's worth. One day after this we saw the French child in the town, seated at a table in the confectioner's with her manager, eating a great many chocolate éclairs with a wan and emotionless face.

During Bajiram,[1] the railways sold return tickets to Cairo at half price, so the solicitor and I went up for a night in a very comfortable pullman carriage. The line runs for some time between the lake and the canal, then, with desert on one side, to Cantara, the junction for Jerusalem and the site of one of the largest base camps of the last war, and then through the Nile valley to Cairo. This last part of the journey was particularly beautiful after the weeks we had spent in the colourless surroundings of Port Said; acres and acres of brilliant green crops stretched out on either side of us, divided by little dykes of running water which blinded oxen filled, pacing round and round the wells in their narrow circle; camels were swaying along the roads, laden with great bundles of vegetation. Everything gave an impression of effortless opulence and biblical fertility. Agriculture on this superb soil is a very different art from that harsh struggle for subsistence among the rocky small holdings of Southern Europe.

We arrived at Cairo in the late afternoon and went to look for an hotel. All the hotels in Egypt are bad, but they excuse themselves upon two contrary principles. Some maintain, legitimately, that it does not really matter how bad they are if they are cheap enough; the others, that it does not really matter how bad they are if they are expensive enough. Both classes do pretty well. We sought out one of the former, a large, old-fashioned establishment under Greek management in the Midan el-Khaznedar, called the Hotel Bristol et du Nil, where rooms even in the high season are only 80 piastres a night. My room had three double beds in it under high canopies of dusty mosquito netting, and two derelict rocking chairs. The windows opened on to a tram terminus. None of the servants spoke

1. I am not sure if this is the most correct spelling of the word. It is pronounced Biram. There seem to be two or three Europeanized spellings for almost every Arabic word.

a word of any European language, but this was a negligible defect since they never answered the bell.

Dennis – as it would be more convenient to name my companion – had been to Cairo before and was anxious to show me the sights, particularly, of course, those of the 'red light district'. We walked along the Sharia el-Genaineh to Shepheard's for cocktails. This street, which runs along one side of the Ezbekiyeh Gardens, is notable for its beggars, who line the railings exhibiting their sores and deformities, and clutching at the clothes of the passers-by. Shepheard's was full of exhausted tourists, just back from their round of sight-seeing. We went on to dinner at the St James's restaurant, which Dennis knowingly called 'Jimmy's'. This is a tolerable imitation of a small English grill-room, with bottles of Worcester sauce, ketchups, and relishes on the tables. After dinner, inevitably, we sought out the houses of ill fame. These all lie in the triangle of slum behind the Sharia el-Genaineh. At their doors and above the entrances to the alleys were pasted notices saying, 'Out of Bounds to all Ranks of H.M. Forces'. The reason for this interdiction, we learned, was not so much to protect the morals or health of the troops as the peace of the inhabitants. Just after the war the Australians, in their fun, threw a young woman to her death out of a top-storey window, and then refused even to pay the normal charges of the establishment. Decent Egyptians refused to frequent places where that kind of thing was likely to occur, so that the brothel-keepers were obliged to seek protection from the military authorities. That, at any rate, was the story we were told.

The whole quarter was brilliantly illuminated in honour of the holiday. Awnings of brightly coloured cotton, printed to imitate carpets, were hung from window to window across the streets. Rows of men and women sat on chairs outside the houses watching the dense crowds who sauntered up and down. Many small cafés were occupied by men drinking coffee, smoking, and playing chess. This district, in addition to its disreputable trade, is the centre of a vivid social life; men were dancing deliberate and rather ungainly folk dances in some of the cafés. There was plenty of music on all sides. Except for a picket of military police, we saw no Europeans; nobody stared at us or embarrassed us in any way, but we felt ourselves out of place in this intimate and jolly atmosphere, like gate-crashers intruding on a schoolroom birthday party. We were just about to go when Dennis met an acquaintance – an Egyptian electrical engineer who had been in the ship with him coming out. He shook us both warmly by the hand and introduced the friend who was with him; they linked their arms with ours and all four of us paraded the narrow street in this way, chatting amicably. The engineer, who had been trained in London for some important post connected with telephones, was very anxious that we should form a good impression of his town, and was alternately boastful and apologetic. Did we find it very dirty? We must not think of them as ignorant people; it was a pity it was a holiday; if we had come at any other time he could have shown us things people never dreamed about in London; did we love a lot of girls in London? He did. He showed us a pocket-book stuffed with photographs of them; weren't they peaches? But we must not think Egyptian girls were ugly. Many had skins as fair as our own; if it had not been a holiday, he could have shown us some beauties.

He seemed a popular young man. Friends greeted him on all sides and he introduced us to them. They all shook hands and offered us cigarettes. As none of them spoke any English these encounters were brief. Finally he asked us if we would like some coffee, and took us into one of the houses.

'This is not so dear as the others,' he explained, 'some of them are terrible what they charge. Just like your London.'

It was called the High Life House, the name being painted up in English and Arabic characters on the door. We climbed a great many stairs and came into a small room where three very old men were playing on oddly shaped stringed instruments. A number of handsomely dressed Arabs sat round the walls munching nuts. They were mostly small landed proprietors, our host explained, up from the country for the festival. He ordered us coffee, nuts, and cigarettes and gave half a piastre to the band. There were two women in the room, a vastly fat white creature of indistinguishable race, and a gorgeous young Sudanese. Would we like to see one of the ladies dance, he asked. We said we would, and suggested the negress. He was puzzled and shocked at our choice. 'She has such a dark skin,' he said.

'We think she is the prettier,' we said.

Courtesy overcame his scruples. After all, we were guests. He ordered the negress to dance. She got up and looked for some castanets without glancing in our direction, moving very slowly. She cannot have been more than seventeen. She wore a very short, backless, red dance dress with bare legs and feet. When she moved it was clear that she had nothing on under her frock. She wore several gold bracelets round her ankles and wrists. These were quite genuine, our host assured us. They always put all their savings into gold ornaments. She found her castanets and began dancing in an infinitely bored way but with superb grace. The more inflammatory her movements became, the more dreamy and detached her expression. There was no suggestion of jazz about her art – merely a rhythmic, sinuous lapsing from pose to pose, a leisurely twisting and vibrating of limbs and body. She danced for a quarter of an hour or twenty minutes, while our host spat nut-shells contemptuously round her feet; then she took up a tambourine and collected money, giving a faintly discernible nod at each donation.

'On no account give her more than half a piastre,' said our host.

I had nothing smaller than a five-piastre piece, so I put that into her collection, but she received it with unmoved indifference. She went out to conceal her winnings and then sat down again, and, taking a handful of nuts, began munching and spitting, her eyes half closed and her head supported on her fist.

Our host was clearly finding us something of an encumbrance by now, so after prolonged exchanges of courtesy and good fellowship we left him for the European quarter. Here we picked up a taxi and told him to drive us to a night club. He took us to one called Peroquet, which was full of young men in white ties throwing paper streamers about. This was not quite what we were looking for, so we drove on right out of the town and across the river to Ghizeh. The place of entertainment here was called Fantasio, and there was a finely liveried commissionaire outside. A number of slot machines in the vestibule, however, removed any apprehensions about its smartness. It was a dreary place. The tables were divided into pens by low wooden partitions; about three quarters of them were empty. On a stage at the end of the hall a young Egyptian was singing what sounded like a liturgical chant in a doleful tenor. With brief pauses, this performance continued as long as we were there. There was a magnificent-looking old sheik in one of the boxes, incapably drunk. (It is all nonsense about Mohammedans not drinking.)

After half an hour of the Fantasio even Dennis's enthusiasm for night life became milder, so we engaged an open horse-carriage and drove back under the stars to the Bristol and Nile. Next day we went out to the scent-makers' bazaar in the Mouski and bought some scent for Juliet, and caught the midday train back to Port Said. We lunched in the pullman and ate, among many other delicacies, some excellent little bitter cucumbers, served hot.

There were many other stimulating and delightful experiences in Port Said – tea at the vicarage, dinner at the consulate, cocktails at Navy House – which approximate too nearly to English life to warrant discussion in a book of travel. There was an evening when the club entertained the wardroom of a visiting battleship; and on that occasion I was slapped on the back, as I entered the bar, by a red-headed youth who said, 'Will you take a drink with the senior service, sir?' What does he know of England who only England knows? When I come to write my novel of Port Said life there will be many such incidents to recount, but for the purpose of this present book only one other episode in my visit deserves mention. That is the trip which Dennis and I took on the Menzaleh canal to a fishing village called Matarieh.

The Menzaleh canal is a term used to dignify the navigable track across the lake from Port Said to Damietta where the bottom has been artificially deepened in places to a few feet, and the shallows marked off with piles. There is daily service down this shallow trough worked by a paddle steamer and a motor launch. Matarieh is a convenient halfway point. One starts at eight in the morning on the steamer and arrives at noon. In an hour the motor launch on its way from Damietta picks one up and takes one back to Port Said by five o'clock. Except for the manager of the canal company, only one other English resident had ever been on this journey; he was the retiring doctor, who, in his first weeks, had set out that way in the hopes of shooting snipe, and had 'collared a jolly good bag, too'.

Mr Bodell gave us sandwiches, and the manager came to see us off from the quay opposite the Maison Dorée. It was a fine, sunny day. The only other first-class passengers were two American missionary women who sat in their cabin sewing. Dennis and I had

77

brought beer, tobacco, and books; the manager lent us two easy chairs from the office.

'Paddle steamer' gives a wrong idea of this boat. It had nothing in common with the floating club-houses of the Nile or the Mississippi except its means of propulsion. This was a single paddle set in the stern, which acted also as a dredger, churning up sand and gravel from the bottom as we went along. Our boat had no name. It was built in two storeys, with a flat roof and flat bottom; it drew about nine inches of water. The lower floor was engine-room, hold, and second-class saloon rolled into one. Twenty or thirty Arabs and Egyptians, men, women, and children, sprawled among heaps of fuel and a cargo of sacks. The top floor was approached by an iron ladder. Here there were two cabins and some breadth of grubby deck. This ship had once been to sea; the manager had brought it himself from Alexandria to Port Said in the first months of the war, with six terrified and seasick Egyptians on board.

The canal led past many flat islands, some mere sand-dunes, others covered with grass. On one there was a large ruined mosque. There were hundreds of little fishing-boats all over the lake, most of them apparently navigated by small boys; they are of identically the same construction as those depicted in hieroglyphic drawings – fish-shaped, with a single sail on a long flexible cross beam and short mast. There were also fishermen wading about with hand nets like those used for shrimping. The catch from this lake are the very tasteless little fish that are inevitable at any Port Said dinner-table. Once or twice we narrowly escaped collision with some of the fishing-boats, and once we ran aground and had to be pushed off by hand. It was a delightful, lazy morning in the sun.

Matarieh seemed very remote indeed from Cairo or Port Said; a little collection of one-storeyed cabins built on a promontory and joined by a strip of railway-line to the mainland. I suppose our arrival there was nearly as surprising as would be the arrival in a Dorset village of an Arab sheik in native costume. At any rate, it created enormous excitement. The clerk of the canal company received us with great courtesy and a few words of English; he bowed us into the hut which served as his office; and gave us each a bag of peanuts and some ginger beer. There was a framed photograph of the Great Pyramid on his desk. We attempted to walk round the village, but soon collected the entire population at our heels. They followed at a few paces' distance, giggling and nudging one another; when we stopped, they stopped; when we turned round and glared at them, they backed away and attempted to take cover. Dennis took a snapshot of them which, unfortunately, failed to develop. Their attitude was certainly not hostile, nor, I think, really derisive; it was merely uncontrolled curiosity of the kind which impels English women to jostle round one as one goes into a wedding, but it was acutely embarrassing, so we returned to the Menzaleh Canal Navigation Company's office, when the agent was most apologetic.

'This is a dirty hole,' he said. 'All full of savage sailors – like in resemblance to your own Malta.' (Those were his exact words. We could all make up remarks of that kind; the only reason why this one is worth recording is that it happens to be genuine.)

Presently the motor launch came to take us back. There was one other passenger with us, a finely dressed Arab with a big gold-topped walking-stick. He was sitting back in the stern seat, eating bread and olives; his four wives and nine or ten children were travelling second class, separated from us by a wicker screen. When he had finished his luncheon he offered some to us, and, when we refused, passed the remains through to them. The women poked henna-stained fingers through the lattice, asking for cigarettes. Dennis was carrying a shooting-stick which attracted his curiosity. He could speak no English, but we demonstrated its use in dumb show. He was delighted and made a little joke, pretending to sit on the nob of his own cane; the chief point of that joke was that he was vastly fat. Two of his wives were squinnying through the grill, and burst out laughing too, but were quickly silenced by some words of reprimand, uttered very sternly in Arabic. When we arrived at Port Said we saw him get into a carriage and drive away, leaving his women to follow on foot with the luggage. A right-minded, high-principled man.

FOUR

Shortly before Easter the doctors pronounced Juliet fit to move, so we packed up and left Port Said for Cairo. Before going we made our adieux to the various people who had befriended us. This was no modern, informal leave-taking, but a very solemn progression from house to house with little packs of calling cards marked 'p.p.c.' in the corner. I had heard scathing comments from time to time at Port Said dinner-parties on people who neglected these polite observances.

The journey was unremarkable except to Juliet, who was not used to the ways of Egyptian porters. These throw themselves upon one's baggage like Westminster schoolboys on their Shrove Tuesday pancake, with this difference, that their aim is to carry away as small a piece as possible; the best fighter struggles out happily with a bundle of newspapers, a rug, an air-cushion, or a small attaché case; the less fortunate share the trunks and suitcases. In this way one's luggage is shared between six or seven men, all of whom clamorously demand tips when they have finally got it into the train or taxi. Juliet was shocked to see her husband and myself defending our possessions from attack with umbrella and walking-stick; when the first onslaught was thus checked and our assailants realized that we had not newly disembarked, we were able to apportion it between two of them and proceed on our way with dignity.

We had booked rooms at Mena House on the grounds that desert air and a certain degree of luxury were essential to Juliet's recovery. It is the one of the grand hotels of Egypt that comes nearest to justifying their terrific charges. Shepheard's, Mena, the Semiramis, the Continental, the Grand Hotel at Heliopolis, the Palace at Luxor, and one or two others are all owned by the same company. Most of them shut for the summer, and the company make it their aim to amass in the four months of the Egyptian high season the profit

which places of more equable climate distribute over the entire year.
Mena seems to me by far the best value. It stands outside the town
beyond Ghizeh, immediately below the Great Pyramid. The road
out to it is a great place for motor-speeding, and there is usually a
racing car or so piled up at the side of the road any time one goes
along, for Egyptians, particularly the wealthier ones, are reckless
with machinery. We passed two on our way out with Juliet, one
about two hundred yards from the road in a field of cucumbers, with
two *fellahin* eyeing it distrustfully. Trams run all the way out to the
pyramids, but they are crowded and slow and are very little used by
Europeans or Americans. At the tram terminus there are a mob of
dragomans, a great number of camels and mules for hire, a Greek-
owned café, a picture-postcard shop, a photographic shop, a curiosity shop specializing in scarabs, and Mena House. This is a large
building in pseudo-Oriental style, standing in a vast and very lovely
garden. When one is paying more than one can really afford, one
is inclined to become over-critical. Mena seemed to me lacking in
most of the things which distinguish a first-rate from a second-rate
hotel; the meals were pretentious and mediocre; there were never
enough pens in the writing-rooms; I wanted another table in my
bedroom and had to make three applications before it appeared;
Juliet had dinner in bed, and instead of bringing up each course
separately, they left them all together on a tray outside her door to
get cold; my bill was made out wrong and the office staff received
the correction ungratefully; there were far too many servants in the
hall and not enough in the bedrooms – I could continue this series
of quite justifiable complaints for some time, but I think it would
make dull reading. We grumbled a good deal while we were there,
but the fact remains that we enjoyed ourselves, and against all the
disadvantages which I have retailed we must set the very great
beauty of the surroundings. On three sides the desert began immediately below the garden wall and stretched out to the horizon in wave
upon wave of sand, broken during the day by miasmas and little
patches of iridescence. The pyramids were a quarter of a mile away,
impressive by sheer bulk and reputation; it felt odd to be living at
such close quarters with anything quite so famous – it was like having
the Prince of Wales at the next table in a restaurant; one kept
pretending not to notice, while all the time glancing furtively to see

if they were still there. The gardens were grossly luxuriant, a mass of harsh greens and violets. Round the house they were studded with beds, packed tight with brilliantly coloured flowers, like Victorian paperweights, while behind and beyond were long walks bordered by gutters of running water, among orchards and flowering trees heavy with almost overpowering scent; there were high cactus hedges and a little octagonal aviary, and innumerable white-robed gardeners, who stood up from their work and bowed and presented buttonholes when a visitor passed them. There was a stable of good horses for hire, besides camels and donkey-carts; there were tennis courts, billiard tables, swimming pool, golf links (among other amenities an English Protestant chapel and chaplain), and, above all, perfectly soundless nights, which one cannot find anywhere in Cairo.

There was also plenty of life, particularly at the weekends. The residents were mostly elderly and tranquil, but for luncheon and tea all kinds of amusing people appeared. Huge personally conducted luxury tours of Americans and northern Englishmen, Australians in *jodhpurs* with topees and fly-whisks, very smart Egyptian officers with vividly painted motor cars and astonishing courtesans – one in a bright green picture frock led a pet monkey on a gold chain; it wore a jewelled bracelet round its neck and fleaed its rump on the terrace while she had her tea. On Easter Monday they had what they called a gymkhana, which meant that all the prices were raised for that afternoon. Apart from this it was not really a success. There was a gentlemen's camel race which was very easily won by an English sergeant who knew how to ride, and a ladies' camel race for which there were no competitors, and a ladies' donkey race won by a noisy English girl of seventeen, and a gentlemen's donkey race for which there were no competitors, and an Arabs' camel race the result of which had clearly been arranged beforehand, and an Arabs' donkey race which ended in a sharp altercation and the exchange of blows. There was an English tourist who tried to make a book; he stood on a chair and was very facetious, but gave such short odds that there were no takers. There was a lady of rank staying in the hotel who gave away the prizes – money to the camel- and donkey-boys and hideous works of Egyptian art to the Europeans. On another evening there was a ball, but that too was ill attended, as it happened to coincide with a reception at the Residency, and no one was anxious to advertise the fact that he had not been invited there.

Geoffrey's and my chief recreations were swimming and camel-riding. We used to ride most days for two hours, making a wide circle through the Arab village and up the ancient track past the Sphinx and the smaller pyramids. It is a delightful way of getting about, combining, as it does, complete security with an exhilarating feeling of eminence. A camel bite leads in most cases to the worst kind of blood-poisoning, and it was a little alarming at first when our mounts turned round and snapped their long green-coated teeth at our knees, but after the first morning we learned to sit cross-legged in the correct Arab fashion, and to guide them with their single hemp reins, while the camel-boys trotted behind and whacked them with a cane. To please their customers, the boys called their beasts by American names – 'Yankydoodle', 'Hitchycoo', 'Red-Hot Momma', etc. They were most anxious to please in every way, even to seizing our hands and foretelling by the lines in our palms illimitable wealth, longevity, and fecundity for both of us.

It was an interesting point of Egyptan commercial organization that a guide hired outside the gates of the hotel cost 8 piastres an hour, while one engaged through the hall porter asked 25 piastres. Geoffrey, Juliet, and I went round the local antiquities with a kindly old bedouin called Solomon, but there is little of interest that has not been taken to the museum at Cairo, as these places were all exca-vated before the modern policy was initiated of leaving relics *in situ*. The pyramids are less impressive when seen close. They are a fine sight from the parapet of the citadel at Cairo, where all five groups of them can be seen standing up in the distinct border of the Nile valley, but, as one approaches, one sees that the original facing has only adhered in a few patches, and the whole now give the impres-sion of immense cairns of stone rather than of buildings. The Sphinx is an ill-proportioned composition of inconsiderable aesthetic ap-peal; and its dramatic value has been considerably diminished since its base was disinterred. The mutilations of its face give it a certain interest. If one had come upon it unexpectedly in some unexplored region, one could be justified in showing mild enthusiasm, but as a piece of sculpture it is hopelessly inadequate to its fame. People from the hotel went out to see it by moonlight and returned very grave and awestruck; which only shows the mesmeric effect of publicity. It is just about as inscrutable and enigmatic as Mr Aleister Crowley.

One Friday, Solomon came to tell us about some religious dances that were to be performed in the neighbourhood; did we want to see them? Juliet did not feel up to it, so Geoffrey stayed at home with her and I went off alone with Solomon. We rode to the farther end of the plateau on which the pyramids stand, and then down into a sandy hollow where there were the entrances to several tombs. Here we left our camels in charge of a boy and climbed into one of the holes in the hillside. The tomb was already half full of Arabs; it was an oblong chamber cut in the rock and decorated in places with incised hieroglyphics. The audience were standing round the walls and packed in the recesses cut for the coffins. The only light came through the door – one beam of white daylight. The moment we arrived the dance began. It was performed by young men, under the direction of a sheik; the audience clapped their hands in time and joined in the chant. It *was* a dull dance, like kindergarten Eurythmics. The youths stamped their feet on the sandy floor and clapped their hands and swayed slowly about. After a short time I signed to Solomon my readiness to leave, and attempted to make as unobtrusive a departure as possible so as not to disturb these ungainly devotions. No sooner, however, had I reached the door than the dance stopped and the whole company came trooping out crying for 'bakshish'. I asked Solomon whether it was not rather shocking that they should expect to be paid by an infidel for keeping their religious observances. He said, rather sheepishly, that some tip was usual to the sheik. I asked where the sheik was. 'Sheik. Me sheik,' they cried, all running forward and beating their chests. Then the old man appeared. I gave him the piastres and they promptly transferred their attention to him, seizing his robes and clamouring for a share. We mounted our camels and rode away. Even then two or three urchins pursued us on foot crying, 'Bakshish! Bakshish! Me sheik!'

As we went back I asked Solomon, 'Was that a genuine religious dance?'

He pretended not to understand.

'You did not like the dance?'

'Would they have done that dance if you had not brought me?'

Solomon was again evasive. 'English and American lords like to see dance. English lords all satisfied.'

'I wasn't satisfied,' I said.

Solomon sighed. 'All right,' he said, which is the Arab's reply to all difficulties with English and American lords. 'Better dance another day.'

'There won't be another day.'

'All right,' said Solomon.

But I did not tell Geoffrey and Juliet it had been a bogus dance. They wished they had come when I told them how interesting it had been.

Another expedition which I made alone was to Sakkara, the enormous necropolis some way down the Nile from Mena. There are two pyramids there, one, rising in steps, which is considerably older than the pyramid at Ghizeh, and a number of tombs; one of them, named unpronounceably the Mastaba of Ptahhotep, is exquisitely decorated in low relief. It is ill-lighted, and a slightly impatient custodian waits on one with candles and magnesium wire; the low ceiling is entirely covered with the initials of tourists written with candle smoke. Another still more beautifully sculptured chamber is called more simply the Mastaba of Ti. As I emerged from this vault I came upon a large party of twenty or thirty indomitable Americans dragging their feet, under the leadership of a dragoman, across the sand from a charabanc. I fell in behind this party and followed them underground again, this time into a vast subterranean tunnel called the Serapeum, which, the guide explained, was the burial-place of the sacred bulls. It was like a completely unilluminated tube railway station. We were each given a candle, and our guide marched on in front with a magnesium flare. Even so, the remote corners were left in impenetrable darkness. On either side of our path were ranged the vast granite sarcophagi; we marched very solemnly the full length of the tunnel, our guide counting the coffins aloud for us; there were twenty-four of them, each so massive that the excavating engineers could devise no means of removing them. Most of the Americans counted aloud with him.

One is supposed, I know, to think of the past on these occasions; to conjure up the ruined streets of Memphis and to see in one's mind's eye the sacred procession as it wound up the avenue of sphinxes, mourning the dead bull; perhaps even to give license to one's fancy and invent some personal romance about the lives of these garlanded hymn-singers, and to generalize sagely about the mutability of human achievement. But I think we can leave all that to Hollywood. For my own part I found the present spectacle infinitely stimulating. What a funny lot we looked, trooping along that obscure gallery! First the Arab with his blazing white ribbon of magnesium, and behind him, clutching their candles, like penitents in procession, this whole rag-tag and bobtail of self-improvement and uplift. Some had been bitten by mosquitoes and bore swollen, asymmetrical faces; many were footsore, and limped and stumbled as they went; one felt faint and was sniffing 'salts'; one coughed with dust; another had her eyes inflamed by the sun; another wore his arm in a sling, injured in heaven knows what endeavour; every one of the party in some way or another was bruised and upbraided by the thundering surf of education. And still they plunged on. One, two, three, four ... twenty-four dead bulls; not twenty-three or twenty-five. How could they remember twenty-four? Why, to be sure, it was the number of Aunt Mabel's bedroom at Luxor. 'How did the bulls die?' one of them asks.

'What did he ask?' chatter the others.

'What did the guide answer?' they want to know.

'How *did* the bulls die?'

'How much did it cost?' asks another. 'You can't build a place like this for nothing.'

'We don't spend money that way nowadays.'

'Fancy spending all that burying bulls ...'

Oh, ladies and gentlemen, I longed to declaim, dear ladies and gentlemen, fancy crossing the Atlantic Ocean, fancy coming all this way in the heat, fancy enduring all these extremities of discomfort and exertion; fancy spending all this money, to see a hole in the sand where, three thousand years ago, a foreign race whose motives must for ever remain inexplicable interred the carcasses of twenty-four bulls. Surely the laugh, dear ladies and gentlemen, is on us.

But I remembered I was a gate-crasher in this party and remained silent.

We often drove into Cairo by the hotel bus and did sight-seeing. We went to the museum. It is some indication of the official Egyptian attitude towards tourists that the price for admission to this collection drops from 10 piastres to one piastre at the end of the Cairo season. The Egyptians have never taken the smallest interest in their antiquities; they have remained an invading race throughout the centuries of their occupation, and have consistently been either neglectful or actively destructive of the civilization of their predecessors. When in the last century European antiquarians, at their own expense and often at considerable personal risk, began excavating and preserving the works of art that had survived the generations of depredation and decay, the Egyptians suddenly woke to the fact that their waste lands contained treasures of the highest commercial value. Even then everything was left to the private enterprise of French and English scholars; Egypt has not produced a single first-rate Egyptologist, contenting herself with the more modest office of fattening on the visitors who came to examine the achievements of their fellow countrymen. So churlish is their attitude, moreover, towards the founders of their prosperity that nowhere in the official catalogue of the Tutankhamen discoveries, nor, so far as I could see, in the galleries themselves, was there any mention of the names of Lord Carnarvon or Mr Howard Carter. In distributing blame, however, it is only fair to credit British commercial enterprise with the gradual erosion by yearly inundation of the lovely little temple of Philae.

The important point about Egyptian works of art, which seems rarely to be appreciated by tourists or archaeologists, is that they really *are* works of art.

There seem to me few things more boring than the cult of mere antiquity. I would view with the utmost equanimity the obliteration of all those cromlechs and barrows and fosses of our remote ancestors which litter the English countryside; whenever I see Gothic lettering on the ordnance survey map I set my steps in a contrary direction. I wish all the rectors who spend their days in scratching up flint arrow-heads and bits of pottery and horrible scraps of tessellated pavement would bury them again and go back to their prayers. But Egyptian antiquities are quite another matter. There is nothing here to evoke that patronizing interest with which we arm ourselves in our surveys of ancient British remains ... How clever of Dr So-and-So to guess that that little splinter of bone in the glass case was not really a little splinter of bone but a Pictish needle – and how clever of the Picts all those years ago to think of making a needle out of a little splinter of bone ... There is nothing of that in our appreciation of Egyptian remains, particularly the incomparable collection recently unearthed in the tomb of Tutankhamen. Here we are in touch with a civilization of splendour and refinement; of very good sculpture, superb architecture, opulent and discreet ornament, and, so far as one can judge, of cultured and temperate social life, comparable upon equal terms with that of China or Byzantium or eighteenth-century Europe, and superior in every artistic form to Imperial Rome or the fashionable cultures of the Minoans or the Aztecs.

The neglect of Egyptian art by the English artistic public seems to me to be due to two causes. One, the very simple one, that the unremitting avarice of the Egyptian race makes it impossible for many people of culture to afford to visit them, and secondly, that the romantic circumstances of the Tutankhamen discovery were so vulgarized in the popular Press that one unconsciously came to regard it less as an artistic event than as some deed of national prowess – a speed record broken, or a birth in the Royal Family; after the discovery came the death of Lord Carnarvon, and the public imagination wallowed in superstitious depths. By the time that adequate photographs began to appear it was impossible to dissociate them from all the irrelevant bubble of emotion and excitement. In the mind of the public the tomb of Tutankhamen became a second Queen's Doll's House full of 'quaint' and 'amusing' toys. The fact that a rich and beautiful woman, even though living very long ago, should still require the toilet requisites of a normal modern dressing-table was greeted with reverberations of surprise and delight and keenly debated controversies in the Press about the variable standards of female beauty. The fact that idle men, very long ago, passed their time in gambling and games of skill was a revelation. Everything of 'human' interest was extensively advertised, while the central fact, that the sum of the world's beautiful things had suddenly been enormously enriched, passed unemphasized and practically unnoticed.

Mr Howard Carter's books and the official catalogue give a complete inventory of the treasures, and there is nothing to be gained by my including here a paraphrase of these accurate and restrained accounts; but I must mention as works of outstanding beauty and nobility the two lifesize figures of the king which were found in the ante-chamber, on either side of the entrance to the sepulchre (cases 5 and 6, Nos. 181 and 96); they are carved in wood and covered partly with gold leaf and partly with black varnish; except for a difference in head-dress they are nearly identical. The king is represented in the act of walking, a tall stick in one hand, a mace in the other; his eyes, gold-lined, stare straight before him; he is travelling with the wind, which blows his skirt tight about his legs at the back and throws it stiffly forward in front. These two figures seem to me unique in sculpture as a perfectly satisfactory statement of the motion of walking. It is interesting to compare them with Mr Tait McKenzie's solution of the same problem in the war memorial at Cambridge.

Next, and second only to these in value, I should put the wooden chest (case 20, No. 324), painted on the top with hunting scenes and on the side panels with battle pictures of the king's victory over his northern and southern enemies, the Asiatics and Nubians. In the brilliant draughtsmanship of these miniatures one sees the sudden flowering into genius of the stiff, scriptural decoration, hitherto regarded as the Egyptians' whole contribution to graphic art. Nothing that I have seen in Persian painting is more vigorously conceived or tactfully disposed than the design of these panels. There is also a carved wooden chair (case 22, No. 3), which seems to me more satisfactory in design and more sensitive in execution than any article of furniture produced in Europe in any age. The jewellery, though made with obvious taste and discretion, seemed to demand less attention than it received; the beds are supremely elegant; the coffins very fine and rich in general effect, but monotonous and uninspired in detail; all the sculpture is admirable, particularly a big dog and some little gilt goddesses; the alabaster vases are not everyone's cup of tea; I thought them a bore, but better judges than me find them delightful. But without illustrations this commentary must become tedious, and has already extended beyond the limits I intended for it. It would be interesting if some publisher or public body would send out Mr Roger Fry or some other cultured and articulate critic to write a review of these works from a purely aesthetic attitude. It seemed to me a collection which ought to form a necessary part of every artistic education.

There is another museum in Cairo devoted to Arab art. It was practically empty on the morning when I visited it, and I was thus enabled to go round at my leisure, undisturbed. It is a much less popular collection among European tourists, and I confess I sympathize with its neglect. To a Western mind there is something particularly stultifying about the succession of intricate geometrical devices that characterize Arab art. The attendants were most amiable. One of them was in charge of a room reconstructed from a medieval Arab dwelling-house. It was his office, whenever a visitor arrived, to switch on the electric lights in the pierced brass lantern and behind the coloured glass windows, and to set the little fountain playing in the middle of the marble floor. This was obviously a source of great pride to him, and he stood bowing and grinning in sympathy with our expressions of delight. The greater part of the collection consists of woodwork – lattices of *mashrabieh* and door panels of inlaid arabesques. There is also a room full of brass lamps, all designed and decorated with the same patience and lack of enterprise; some incised plaster work; some leather book-bindings, and a little pottery.

I was moved by something of the Crusader's zeal for cross against crescent, as I reflected that these skilful, spiritless bits of merchandise were contemporary with the Christian masterpieces of the Musée Cluny. The period of Arab supremacy in Egypt coincides almost exactly with the dominion of Latin Christianity in England; during those centuries when the Christian artists were carving the stalls of our cathedrals and parish churches, these little jigsaw puzzles were being fitted together beyond the frontiers, by artificers whose artistic development seemed to have been arrested in the kindergarten stage, when design meant metrical symmetry and imagination the endless alternative, repetition, and regrouping of the same invariable elements. Living as we are under the impact of the collective inferiority complex of the whole West, and humbled as we are by the many excellencies of Chinese, Indians, and even savages, we can still hold up our heads in the Mohammedan world with the certainty of superiority. It seems to me that there is no single aspect of Mohammedan art, history, scholarship, or social, religious, or political organization, to which we, as Christians, cannot look with unshaken pride of race.

The Arabs come nearest, perhaps, to exciting our admiration, in their architecture. Driving about the streets of the old town we continually came upon buildings of great sweetness and attraction – squat onion-shaped domes; high pointed domes like Saracen helmets; white minarets like wedding-cake decorations or ornamental bone penholders; little white-washed courtyards with trees growing in them and fountains; great stone doorways canopied with stalactite vaulting; fretted plaster façades; cloisters with gilded and painted beams; balconies screened from the street with black *mashrabieh*; ruined tombs silted up with sand; vast, densely populated courts with mosaic walls and pavement – all these make a direct but somewhat superficial appeal to our affections. I tried to go round the principal mosques in an intelligent and critical manner, but found that there was too much to assimilate that was odd and unfamiliar. I began to sympathize with American visitors to Europe. We, who have grown up in lifelong familiarity with a mature culture, have, to some extent, an instinctive discrimination of the genuine from the spurious in our own civilization. We can perceive uncertainty in an artistic motive; we know when an idea is new and vital and when the artist has become bored, imitative, and repetitive. We do not confuse nineteenth- with thirteenth-century Gothic; we can relate the art of our own continent to its history; heraldry and ecclesiastical symbolism throw out allusions which we can recognize. To those who are born in a new country and brought up among half-finished institutions, three hundred years ago is much the same as five hundred; one cathedral much the same as another, be it Norman, Gothic, or Baroque; one Virgin and Child much the same as another, be it by Cimabue, Filippo Lippi, or Mantegna. The date in the guide book, four numerals in a row, is unrelated to the fact, and therefore hard to remember, easy to confuse ludicrously. 'Did you say B.C. or A.D.?' is quite a common question from tourist to guide.

In just this way I found myself floundering hopelessly in my attempts to grasp the essentials of Arab architecture. I would memorize a list of dynasties and dates in the morning and forget them before luncheon; I confused the features of one building with those of another, and, looking at photographs later, was often unable to remember which buildings I had seen and which I had not. It would clearly take more than the three weeks at my disposal to get any kind of coherent impression, so in the end I was content to give up the attempt, treating the places we visited as so many spots of natural beauty. In this way I passed the time pleasantly if unprofitably.

One of the religious buildings which interested me most was the University of El Azhar, the centre of Moslem scholarship. Moslem scholarship consists in learning by heart long passages of theology. El Azhar is a large establishment, dating from the early fourteenth century, with more than ten thousand students of all ages and nationalities, and three or four hundred dons. We watched some of them at work, squatting, packed together, in a vast, pillared hall, rocking on their heels and repeating with half-closed eyes verse after verse of the Koran. Even Oxford seemed comparatively vital by contrast.

The citadel, too, repaid the precipitous ascent. The alabaster mosque of Mohammed Ali is enormous and vulgar, like a music-hall, but there is an arresting cast-iron fountain in the outer court, presented by Louis Philippe; there is also a charming deserted palace, the site of the murder of the Mamluks, with nineteenth-century mural decorations in grisaille. The view across Cairo to Ghizeh and the Nile valley, with the groups of pyramids clearly standing out against the desert, and the hundreds of domes and minarets bristling out of the city at one's feet, is a memorable experience.

As I wished to see a little more of Egypt before leaving, I drove down to Helwan for a couple of nights. It is an inconsiderable cluster of villas and hotels existing simply for the spa. I stayed in an excellent English *pension*, called the English Winter Hotel; the beds in the garden were edged with bottles; there were two lemurs in cages; the other guests were a colonel, two bishops, and an archdeacon, all very British. Before I had been there two hours I knew everything there was to know about their rheumatism.

The road from Helwan to Cairo runs along the Nile bank past a large convict settlement, a very palatial royal villa, and an ancient Coptic church, and enters Cairo through a very interesting quarter which many tourists omit to visit. That is Masr el Atika, Old Cairo or Babylon, the Coptic settlement built in the days of persecution within the walls of the old Roman garrison station. In this constricted slum there are five medieval Coptic churches, a synagogue, and a Greek Orthodox convent. The Christians seem to differ in decency very little from their pagan neighbours; the only marked sign of their emancipation from heathen superstition was that the swarm of male and juvenile beggars were here reinforced by their womenfolk, who in the Mohammedan quarters maintain a modest seclusion. The churches, however, were most interesting, particularly Abu Sergh, which has Corinthian columns taken from a Roman temple, Byzantine eikons, and an Arabic screen. It is built over the cave where the Holy Family – always troglodytic – are said to have spent their retirement during Herod's massacre of the innocents. The deacon, Bestavros, showed us over. When he had finished his halting exposition and received his tip, he said, 'Wait one minute. Get priest.'

He hurried into the vestry and brought out a patriarchal old man with a long grey beard and large greasy bun of grey hair, obviously newly awakened from his afternoon nap. This priest blinked, blessed us, and held out his hand for a tip; then, lifting up his skirts, he tucked the two piastres away in a pocket and made off. At the vestry door he stopped. 'Go getting bishop,' he said.

Half a minute later he returned with a still more venerable figure, chewing sunflower seeds. The pontiff blessed us and held out his hand for a tip. I gave him two piastres. He shook his head.

'He is a bishop,' explained Bestavros, 'three piastres for a Bishop.'

I added a piastre and he went away beaming. Bestavros then sold me a copy of a history of the church written by himself. It is such a very short work that I think it worth reproducing here with spelling and punctuation exactly as it was printed.

A BRIEF HISTORY

of

ABU SARGA CHURCH

By

MESSIHA BESTAVROS

ABU SARGA CHURCH

This Church was built in the year A.D. 1171 by a man whose name was Hanna El Abbah the secretary of Sultan Salah-El-Din El-Ayoubi.

The Church contains 11 marble pillars each containing a panting of one of the apostles and one granite pillar without capital, panting or cross alladvig Judes who betrayed our Lord.

The alter for the holy comminion contains 7 Maszaic steps (the 7 degrees of bishops). The screen of the alter is made of carved ivory.

On the North of wich were are tow nice penals of carved wood: one shows the last supper and the other Bethlehm. On there Southern sides St Demetrius, St Georges and St Theodore.

The cript was cut out of a solid rock 30 years B.C. Mearly which was used as a shelter for strangers. When the Holy Family moved from Jernsalim to Egypt to hide themselves from King Herod they found this cript where they remained until the death of King Herod.

When St Mark started preaching in Alexandria at 42 A.D. and we the Pharos who embraced the religion of Christ used this criot as a church for a period of 900 years till this church built on its top. On the other side of the cript you can see the fount where Christian children are baptised by emersion in water for 3 times. This church contains many Byzantian painitings of the 9th & 10th centuries.

MEISHA BESTAVROS,
Deacon

Opposite old Babylon is Roda Island, with a p… ;, derelic. garden and an old Nilometer.

FIVE

I parted from Geoffrey and Juliet at Port Said. They had cabled to Juliet's sister for more money and, as soon as it arrived, set off for Cyprus in a Khedivial Line ship. She left late at night, and I saw them off and drank some vermouth with them in a gaily upholstered saloon; the ship was coaling at the time and everything was slightly grimy; the other passengers were Greeks. I had to climb across two coal barges to get back to my boat. As we rowed back across the harbour, whose black waters reflected row upon row of bright portholes where the big ships lay at anchor, and whose air echoed with the singing of the coolies and the shouts of the porters and boatmen and the howling of the dredgers, my meditations were disturbed by a vigorous attempt on the part of the two oarsmen to blackmail me into increasing the price we had already agreed upon for the journey. They stopped rowing and we drifted about in the dark, arguing. I had learned an Arabic phrase which sounded like '*Ana barradar*'. I do not know what it meant, but I had used it once or twice in Cairo with fair success. I kept repeating it at intervals during the conversation. In the end they started rowing again and, when we reached the shore, I gave them their original price. It was interesting to notice that they bore no malice about it, but sent me away with smiles and bows and the entreaty that I would use their boat again (which was painted on the back seat with a U.S. flag and the title 'Gene Tunney'). This very sensible attitude seemed to show the advantages of not having an inherited Protestant conscience. When an Englishman attempts to be extortionate and fails, he keeps up his grumble until one is out of earshot, and, I believe, does bear a genuine personal grudge against one for the rest of that day. He does not admit, even to himself, that he was 'trying it on' or accept defeat with good grace. Arabs and, I imagine, most Oriental races, have no conception of the 'fair price' or of absolute values of exchange.

95

Hence, no doubt, the Jews' superiority over Europeans in finance. The English boatman prefers to kick his heels day after day on the quayside, rather than take less for his labour than he has convinced himself is right. He very rarely attempts to get more, even if his passengers look rich and their need for his service acute. When he does, it is only after convincing himself that the increased demand is actually the normal one. When he is caught out his conclusion is that his customer was no gentleman to make such a fuss about a shilling. It is the same with writers, who will all gladly starve their wives and tailors rather than accept less than their fifteen guineas a thousand words, while at the same time maintaining an undertone of complaint against the ignorance and meanness of editors and publishers.

Next day I, too, left Port Said in the P. & O. ship *Ranchi* for Malta. On leaving Egypt, as a final nip of avarice, one is obliged to pay a few shillings 'quarantine tax'. I should have paid a similar levy on landing, but, as I came off the *Stella*, no one asked me for it. Accordingly I had to pay double on leaving. No one seems to know anything about this imposition, what statute authorized it and how much of what is collected ever finds its way into the treasury, or what bearing it has upon 'quarantine'. Many residents maintain that it is purely a bit of fun on the part of the harbour officials, who have no legal right to it whatever. Anyway, it seems to me a model of revenue collection, as the sum is not large enough to raise protests from any but the most truculent and is demanded when delay is least desirable, just when one is most harassed with getting one's luggage through the customs, catching trains or boats, and landing in a new country.

Thanks to the kind offices of the local manager, I was able to obtain a second-class berth. The residents in Port Said said: 'You meet a first-rate lot of people travelling second class since the war. A jolly sight better than in the first class, particularly on the ships from India – the first class is all *nouveaux riches*. You meet some pretty rough diamonds in the Australian ships. But you'll find second class on the *Ranchi* as good as first class on a foreign line. My wife travels second class when she goes home.'

But my motive really was less the ambition to meet nice people than to save money. As it was, the second-class fare – twelve pounds for the two days' voyage to Malta – seemed extremely expensive.

After my extravagances at Mena House I was beginning to get worried again about money, so I thought of what still seems to me an ingenious device. Before leaving Cairo I wrote – on the notepaper of the Union Club, Port Said – to the managers of the two leading hotels in Valletta, the Great Britain and the Osborne, between whom, I was told, there existed a relationship of acute rivalry, and enclosed a publisher's slip of Press cuttings about my last book; I said to each that I proposed to publish a travel diary on my return to England; I had heard that his was the best hotel in the island. Would he be willing to give me free accommodation during my visit to Malta in return for a kind reference to his establishment in my book? They had not had time to answer by the time I embarked at Port Said, but I went on board hoping that at Valletta I should experience some remission of the continual draining of money that I had suffered for the last two months.

It is one of the unsatisfactory things about ships that you never know when they are going to arrive. The *Ranchi* was advertised to sail some time on Sunday and was expected early in the afternoon. On Sunday morning she was announced for nine o'clock that evening. Finally she came in well after midnight and stayed only two hours. During those two hours the town, which, as usual, was feeling the ill-effects of its Saturday night at the Casino, suddenly woke again into life. Simon Arzt's store opened; the cafés turned on their lights and dusted the tables; out came the boot-cleaners and postcard sellers; the passengers who had stayed on board through the canal came ashore and drove round in two-horse carriages; those who had left the ship at Aden for a few hours at Cairo, and had spent all that afternoon on the quay in a fever of apprehension that they might miss her, scuttled on board to their cabins; half the residents of Port Said had business of some kind to transact on board. I went down to the harbour in a bustle that was like noon in the City of London. I am quite sure that I have never spent a more boring four hours in my life than those between dinner and the arrival of the *Ranchi*, sitting with my luggage in the deserted hall of Bodell's *pension*. The sudden brightness of the streets and the animation on all sides seemed quite unreal. I went on board, found my steward and my cabin, disposed of my luggage, and went on deck for a little. The passengers who had done the Aden–Cairo–Port Said dash were drinking coffee, eating sandwiches, and describing the pyramids and Shepheard's Hotel. 'Two pounds ten, simply for a single bed and no bathroom. Think of that!' they said with obvious pride. 'And we rode on camels – you should just have seen me. How Katie would have laughed, I said. And the camel-boy told my fortune, and we had a coffee made actually in the temple of the Sphinx. You *ought* to have come. Well, yes, perhaps it was a little exhausting, but then we've plenty of time at sea to make up for it. And there was the sweetest little boy who cleaned our shoes. And we went into a mosque where the Moham-medans were all saying their prayers – so quaint. And would you believe it – at Shepheard's they charged 15 piastres – that's over three shillings – for a cup of early morning tea, and not very good tea at that. You *ought* to have come, Katie!'

Before we sailed, I went down to my cabin and went to bed. The man who was sharing it with me, a kindly, middle-aged, civil engineer, was already undressing; he wore combinations. I woke once when the engines started, dozed and woke again as we ran clear of the breakwater and began to roll, and then fell soundly asleep, to wake next morning on the high seas with a hundred Englishmen all round me, whistling as they shaved.

We had cold, sunless weather and fairly heavy seas during the next two days. I rather wished that I had gone first class. It was not that my fellow passengers were not every bit as nice as the Port Said residents had told me they would be, but that there were so many of them. There was simply nowhere to sit down. The lounge and smoking-room were comfortable and clean and well ventilated and prettily decorated and all that, but they were always completely full. On the decks there were no deck-chairs except those the passengers provided for themselves; the three or four public seats were invariably occupied by mothers doing frightful things to their babies with jars of vaseline. It was not even possible to walk round with any comfort, so confined and crowded was the single promenade deck. It is impossible to walk happily on a rolling ship unless one has ready access to one or other rail for support, and these were always lined with military men in overcoats. Children were everywhere. It was the beginning of the hot season in India, and the officers' wives were taking them back to England in shoals; the better sort lay and cried in perambulators; the worse ones fell all over the deck and were sick;

these ones, too, appeared in the dining-room for breakfast and luncheon and were encouraged by their mothers to eat. There was an awful hour every evening at about six o'clock, when the band came down from the first-class deck to play Gilbert and Sullivan to us in the saloon; this visitation coincided exactly with the bathing of the elder children below; the combination of soap and salt water is one of the more repugnant features of sea travel, and the lusty offspring of sahib and memsahib shrieked their protest till the steel rafters and match-board partitions echoed and rang. There was no place above or below for a man who values silence.

Apart from the overcrowding, the second-class accommodation on the *Ranchi* was, as they had said, a great deal better than the first-class of many ships. The cabins were comfortable, the food unpretentious and wholesome, and one only had to have the band for one hour in the day. The other passengers were mostly soldiers on leave or soldiers' wives, leavened with a few servants of first-class passengers, some clergymen, and three or four nuns. The valets wore neat blue suits throughout the voyage, but the soldiers had an interesting snobbism. During the day, though cleanly shaved and with carefully brushed hair, they cultivated an extreme freedom of dress, wearing khaki shorts and open tennis shirts and faded cricket blazers. At dinner, however, they all appeared in dinner-jackets and stiff shirts. One of them told me that the reason he travelled second class was that he need not trouble about clothes, but that he had to draw the line somewhere. On the other side of the barrier we could see the first-class passengers dressed very smartly in white flannels and parti-coloured brown and white shoes. Among them there was a youth who knew me hurrying back to contest a seat in the Conservative interest at the General Election. He kept popping over the rail to have cocktails with me and tell me about the lovely first-class girls he danced and played quoits with. He cost me quite a lot in cocktails. He often urged me to come over and see all the lovely girls and have cocktails with him. 'My dear chap,' he used to say, 'no one will dare to say anything to you while you're with *me*. I'd soon fix it up with the Captain if they did.' But I kept to my own bar. Later this young man, in his zeal to acquit himself splendidly before the first-class girls, clambered up one of the davits on the boat deck. He was reported to the Captain and seriously reprimanded. P. & O. ships are full of public school spirit. He did very badly indeed in the election, I believe, reducing an already meagre Conservative poll almost to extinction.

Just before luncheon on the third morning, we came in sight of Malta. There was some delay about landing because one of the passengers had developed chicken-pox. There was only one other passenger disembarking. We had to go and see the medical officer in the first-class saloon. He had infinite difficulties about the pronunciation of my name. He wanted to know the address I was going to in Malta. I would only tell him that I had not yet decided between the two hotels. He said, 'Please decide now. I have to fill in this form.'

I said I could not until I had seen the managers.

He said, 'They are both good hotels, what does it matter?'

I said, 'I want to get in free.'

He thought I was clearly a very suspicious character, and told me that on pain of imprisonment, I must report daily at the Ministry of Health during my stay at Valletta. If I did not come the police would find me and bring me. I said I would come, and he gave me a quarantine form to keep. I lost the form that evening and never went near the Ministry of Health and heard no more about it.

We went ashore in a lighter and landed at the Custom House. Here I was met by two young men, both short, swarthy, and vivacious, and each wearing a peaked cap above a shiny English suit. One had 'The Osborne Hotel' in gold on his cap, the other 'The Great Britain Hotel'. Each held in his hand a duplicate letter from me, asking for accommodation. Each took possession of a bit of my luggage and handed me a printed card. One card said:

THE OSBORNE HOTEL
STRADA MEZZODI
Every modern improvement. Hot water. Electric light.
Excellent cuisine.
**PATRONISED BY H.S.H. PRINCE LOUIS OF BATTENBERG
AND THE DUKE OF BRONTE.**

The other said:

THE GREAT BRITAIN HOTEL
STRADA MEZZODI
Every modern improvement. Hot and cold water. Electric light.
Unrivalled cuisine. Sanitation.
THE ONLY HOTEL UNDER ENGLISH MANAGEMENT

(a fact, one would have thought, more fit to be concealed than advertised).

I had been advised in Cairo that the Great Britain was really the better of the two, so I directed its representative to take charge of my luggage. The porter of the Osborne fluttered my letter petulantly before my eyes.

'A forgery,' I explained, shocked at my own duplicity. 'I am afraid that you have been deluded by a palpable forgery.'

The porter of the Great Britain chartered two little horse-carriages, conducted me to one, and sat with the luggage in the other. There were low, fringed canopies over our heads so that it was impossible to see out very much. I was aware of a long and precipitous ascent, with many corners to turn. At some of these I got a glimpse of a baroque shrine, at others a sudden bird's-eye view of the Grand Harbour, full of shipping, with fortifications beyond. We went up and round, along a broad street of shops and more important door-ways. We passed groups of supremely ugly Maltese women wearing an astonishing black head-dress, half veil and half umbrella, which is the last legacy to the island of the conventual inclinations of the Knights of St John. Then we turned off down a narrow side street and stopped at the little iron and glass porch of the Great Britain Hotel. A little dark passage led into a little dark lounge, furnished like an English saloon bar, with imitation leather armchairs, bowls of aspidistra on fumed oak stands, metal topped tables, and tables with plush coverings, Benares brass work, framed photographs, and ash-trays stamped with the trade-marks of various brands of whisky and gin. It was an old house, how old I cannot say, but certainly not later than the middle of the eighteenth century, and its construc-tion seemed in conflict with this scheme of decoration. Do not mistake me; it was not remotely like an old-fashioned hotel in an English market town; it was a realization of the picture I have always in my mind of the interiors of those hotels facing on to Paddington station, which advertise '5s. Bed and Breakfast' over such imposing names as Bristol, Clarendon, Empire, etc. My heart fell rather as I greeted my host in this dingy hall, and continued to fall as I ascended, storey by storey, to my bedroom. The worst of it, however, was in this first impression, and I think I am really doing my duty honourably to the proprietor in warning people of it and exhorting them not to be deterred. For I can quite conscientiously say that the Great Britain *is* the best hotel in the island. There are no luxurious hotels. I went later to look at the Osborne and felt that I had done one better than H.S.H. Prince Louis of Battenberg and the Duke of Bronte. The food at the Great Britain was good; there was a large variety of wine and spirits; the lavatories and bathrooms quite adequate; the servants particularly willing and engaging. As an example of good service I may quote that one evening, being tired and busy, I decided to dine in my room. At Mena House, where there were hosts of servants and a lift, as I have noted, the dinner was brought up in one load and left outside the door; at the Great Britain every course was carried separately up three flights of stairs by the panting but smiling *valet de chambre*.

Before I left, the proprietor of the hotel asked me, rather suspiciously, what I intended to say about him. I replied that I would recommend him to the readers of my book.

They had had another writer, he told me, who had come to stay as his guest; he wrote for a paper called *Town and Country Life*; he had written a very nice piece indeed about the Great Britain. They had had the article reprinted for distribution.

The proprietor gave me a copy.

That, he said, was the kind of article that did a house good. He hoped mine would be as much like that as I could make it.

It was a funny article. It began: 'The beautiful and prolific foliage, exotic skies, and glorious blue waters, a wealth of sunshine that spells health and happiness, and the facilities for enjoying outdoor sports, all the year round, are a few of the reasons that has made Malta so popular. Picturesque scenery, and people, complete as fascinating an array of attractions as the heart of the most blasé, could wish for.' It continued in this way for a column, with the same excess of punctuation; then it gave a brief survey of Maltese history and a description of the principal sights, for another column. Then it started on the Great Britain Hotel. 'No expense,' it said, 'has been spared to make the Public Rooms as comfortable as possible . . . the Management boasts that its meals equal in the excellence of its food, cooking and serving, those served at London's hostelries and restaurants . . . special pains are taken to see that all beds are most comfortable and only best material used . . .' and so on for a column and a half. It finished with this sentence: 'The luxuries of modern civilization have all been embodied in the building and organization of the Great Britain Hotel, Valletta, Malta, where the visitor is able to revel in the joys of a healthy happy stay amidst the fascinations of a modern palace set in Nature's own setting of sea and foliage, and here are to be obtained sunshine and warmth the whole year round.'

I will not be outdone in gratitude. If my appreciation is more temperately expressed it is none the less genuine. Let me state again, the Great Britain may be less suitably placed for golfers than Gleneagles; the bathing may be better from the Normandie; one can shop more conveniently from the Crillon, the Russie is set in a prettier square, one meets more amusing company at the Cavendish, one can dance better at the Berkeley and sleep better at Mena and eat better at the Ritz, but *the Great Britain Hotel, Valletta, Malta, is the best on the island*; further comparisons seem rather to confuse the issue.

Malta was quite different from what I had imagined. I expected it to be much more British and much more breezy. I expected a great many white flag-staffs and bandstands and very clean streets, and officers' wives with Sealyham terriers, and white-washed buildings with verandahs and little brass cannon and lookout towers with spiral iron staircases. I did not associate in my mind a naval base with baroque architecture, and, without giving much thought to it, I supposed the sailors were illimitably supplied with English nursery maids to walk with along the front and take to the cinema; it was odd to see them swaggering down precipitous alleys with prostitutes who talked a mixture of Arabic and Italian. I expected to find a Sabbath-keeping, undemonstrative Protestantism, one English church full of fairly recent memorial tablets, and a chaplain or two carrying tennis rackets. I found the most ardently Catholic people in Europe; a place where the Church owns a third of the soil, and monks, nuns, priests, novices, prelates, and religious processions emerge in serried masses at every corner. I daresay things seem different when the fleet is in; while I was there the harbour was empty except for a submarine, a target carrier, and the usual mercantile shipping. In these circumstances I got the impression of a place far less British than Port Said. It is true that I saw a cricket match being played, and that Gieves have a shop in Strada Mezzodi,

and that notices are displayed at the Custom House and the railway
station advertising the addresses of the local secretaries of the Society
for the Prevention of Cruelty to Animals and the Girls' Friendly
Society, and that English money is used, and that the *cafés chantants*
call themselves music-halls, and that instead of cafés there are public
houses with a row of handles behind the bar and barmaids who draw
up pint glasses of metallic-tasting draught bitter, but in spite of all
this there seemed something superficial about the British occupation.
After all, we have only been there for a little over a hundred years,
and we came, not as colonists among savages, but as the mandatories
of an outpost of high European culture. But trivial as has been the
English influence to alter the essentially Mediterranean character of
the island, this tenancy by a first-class naval power has been the
means of preserving almost the whole of its charm. Malta in the
nineteenth century might so easily have become neutralized and
internationalized, or, worse still, the Order of St John might have
been reconstituted on an archaic-heraldic-churchy basis and the
island have lapsed into bogus autonomy as a carefully nurtured
'quaint survival'. Nothing, of course, could destroy its importance
as a sea port and coaling station, but the three lovely towns of the
Grand Harbour, Valletta, Senglea, and Vittoriosa, might very easily
indeed have fallen to the water-colour artists. They have all the
ingredients of the picturesque – ancient buildings, fortifications,
narrow and precipitous streets, national costume, local religious
festivals, and an unconscionably romantic history; the climate would
have proved very much more favourable to retired aesthetes than the
Riviera; only the acquisitive instincts of British nineteenth-century
diplomacy saved Malta from developing into such a thing as does
not bear thinking of – a nightmare island combining and epitomizing
all the unendurable characteristics of Capri, Rye, and Carcassonne.
The occupation by the British Navy has prevented all that; the
fortifications have not been allowed to crumble and grow mossy;
they are kept in good order, garrisoned and, whenever it was expe-
dient, ruthlessly modified; roads have been cut through them and
ditches filled up. Nothing, except the one museum in the Auberge
d'Italie, has been allowed to become a show place; everything is put
to a soundly practical purpose. There is a governor in the Grand
Master's Palace, monks in the monasteries, marines and naval

officials in the principal houses, a police station in the Knights' Hospital, a modern signalling station perched on the roof of the Auberge de Castille.

I spent too little time in Malta, and look forward eagerly for an opportunity to revisit it. Most of my days were spent in exploring Valletta, with the aid of a small book called *Walks in Malta*, by F. Weston, which I bought for two shillings at Critien's, the big stationer's shop. I found it a slightly confusing book at first until I got used to the author's method; after that I became attached to it, not only for the variety of information it supplied, but for the amusing Boy-Scout game it made of sight-seeing. 'Turning sharply to your left you will notice ...' Mr Weston prefaces his comments, and there follows a minute record of detailed observations. On one occasion, when carrying his book, I landed at the Senglea quay, taking it for Vittoriosa, and walked on for some time in the wrong town, hotly following false clues and identifying 'windows with fine old mould-ings', 'partially defaced escutcheons', 'interesting iron-work balu-strades', etc. for nearly quarter of a mile, until a clearly non-existent cathedral brought me up sharp to the realization of my mistake.

Valletta is built on a high peninsula between two deep creeks which form the natural harbours of Marasmuscetto and the Grand Harbour; the south-east bank of the latter is broken by three smaller and narrower creeks which throw out, at right angles to Valletta, the two peninsulas on which are built the towns of Vittoriosa and Senglea. The north-west bank of the Marsamuscetto Harbour is again broken by creeks into two peninsulas; Forts Tigné and Manoel stand on these points; Fort St Elmo at the head of Valletta and Fort St Angelo at Vittoriosa. Thus, wherever one walks upon the high ground and cavaliers of Valletta, one is confronted with a magnifi-cent prospect of water, shipping, a high and broken coastline, fortifications, and behind these again the rising hills of the interior.

A ferry plies regularly between the three towns. There is very little to see at Senglea except the view it affords of the other two and a delightful sixteenth-century observation tower carved with a huge eye and ear. Vittoriosa has a fine main street with a good deal of Norman work here and there among the houses, a large convent with one of the links which bound St Lawrence to his grid-iron, a bishop's palace and an inquisitor's palace, a good Renaissance church, but the most interesting thing is the disposal of the streets in relation to the fortifications. Vittoriosa is much older than Valletta and was planned in the days of bow and arrow; for this reason the streets that lead inwards from the walls to the centre of the town afford the assaulting party no opportunity for a single victorious charge, but turn backwards and forwards at right angles, each turn a bow-shot from the last, so that the retreating defenders could loose a flight of arrows and instantly take cover, reload, wait the appearance of their enemies, fire again, and again take cover. (All this was explained to me by Mr Weston.)

Valletta was built to withstand bombardment with fire-arms, and is a model of seventeenth-century military science. I should imagine that even today it would be impregnable to infantry until it had first been pounded to pieces from the air or sea. When Napoleon took it, by treachery, his chief of staff is said to have remarked to him, 'It is well, general, that there was someone within to open the gates to us. We should have had trouble in working our way through had the place been empty.'

With Mr Weston's help it is amusing to trace out the particular purpose of each rampart and ditch and cavalier, but the chief interests in Valletta are artistic. Until the beginning of the eighteenth century the Knights of St John were enormously wealthy; at the time of their dissolution they were practically bankrupt and had already been obliged to dispose of some of their treasures; Napoleon's troops carried away most of what was left and lost it in Aboukir Bay, but, in spite of this wholesale depredation, the residue is dazzling in its splendour.

It is hard to form any temperate idea of the magnificence of the Knights' lives in the seventeenth and eighteenth centuries, when even the common sailors in hospital ate off silver plate. It must be remembered that in Malta alone of the cultured states of Europe slave labour was extensively employed for all public works. Mohammedan prisoners, with shaved heads and pig-tails, worked in the quarries and on the fortifications and were herded at night into a common prison. The Knights were an international aristocracy curiously combining the careers of monk and soldier of fortune. One wonders what odd rites of initiation were practised in the Auberges; what friendships and jealousies sprang up among these celibate warriors.

If only there had been some Maltese Guardi or Longhi or Canaletto to record the life of the island for us. It is in the Cathedral of St John, the conventual church of the order, that one gets most idea of its original splendour. This is not a wholly attractive building. Outside it is austere and almost shabby; inside there is no single spot where the eye can rest for one moment that is not ablaze with decoration. The barrel vaulting of the roof is frescoed by Mattia Preti with a series of rich and vigorous baroque compositions. His work was new to me at this time, though since then I have encountered his name repeatedly. He has fearlessly attacked the problem set by the curvature of the surface and has worked prodigies of perspective, enhancing his effects by painting false shadows across the mouldings between the bays. Malta is full of his work, but the ceiling of St John's is by far the grandest and best preserved.

Gafa, the sculptor, is another artist whom I had not heard of before. Indeed, to the best of my knowledge there is no work of his outside the island. I saw a lovely, effeminate head of St John by him and a terrific marble group of the Baptism of our Lord. He died before this was finished and the final touches were left to Bernini, who was engaged on the high altar. There is also a fine Caravaggio in the church, which the verger points out as being by Michael Angelo.

The floor is completely carpeted with the inlaid marble tombstones of the more august knights; there are more than four hundred of them, all heraldic and rococo, many with figures of death as supporters. All round the church are the chapels of the different Languages, most of them with elaborate marble altars and canopies. There is not one piece of plain stone left in the building. The parts of the wall that are not overlaid with marble are carved in high relief with rather boring decorative panels which give an effect of sculptured lodging-house wallpaper. The Chapel of the Language of Auvergne has massive silver gates and screen which escaped pillage by Napoleon through their being painted black and taken for iron. Among its other treasures the cathedral owns a piece of the true cross, a thorn from the crown of thorns, and some of the finest tapestry in Europe, which is only brought out on a few days of the year – alas, on none of the days of my visit.

Another sight to which I was denied access was the Dominican

Chapel of Bones at the end of the town. Apparently some midshipmen had played bowls with the skulls, so the building was locked up even from more responsible visitors. It was possible to obtain an order to view it, I was told, but I felt ashamed to apply, having no possible business there beyond casual curiosity.

I discovered two interesting quarters of Malta for myself. One was the district at the end of the Strada Reale below the Castle of St Elmo, where the seamen go for their recreation. It was full of brilliantly painted public houses and *cafés chantants*. In the absence of the fleet everything was very quiet, but I should think it would repay a visit at a more popular time.

The other must, I should think, be the most concentrated and intense slum in the world. It is called the Manderaggio and consists of a huge pit quarried out on the north-west edge of the town. It was intended originally for an artificial land-locked creek for the protection and repair of small boats, but the work was abandoned before it reached sea level. In this crater the poorest of the population have made their home for the last three hundred years. It is approached from the west end of the Strada San Giovanni, down stone steps under a low arch that reminds one of the Adelphi Arches in London. Until quite recent years it was a place where the police could offer no protection; since then it has been scoured clean of its more militant criminality and it is about as safe as the *vieux port* at Marseilles. It is wise to go with some kind of escort, however, as none of the inhabitants speak a word of any European language, and the labyrinth of streets is so intricate that only those whose families have inhabited it for generations have any sense of its geography. Not a single street in the Manderaggio is accessible to wheeled traffic; most of them are narrow passages in which two can barely pass without brushing against each other; many of them are mere tunnels and flights of steps, roofed over with dwelling-houses; half of them are blind alleys leading through infinite deviations, round hair-pin bends, and up and down precipitous inclines to a dead stop; the houses are jumbled, literally, on top of each other and densely populated; some of them are caves cut in the face of the cliff, some are poised on buttresses over a drop of a hundred feet, some are in cellars approached by steps from the level of the gutter; needless to say, the dirt and smell are overpowering. As is the case with most slums the population seems to consist solely of the extremely young and the extremely old. I suppose that all the active men are down in the harbour. I did not attempt a visit after dark, when, I suppose, the real life of the Manderaggio begins. I am keeping that and the sailor quarter for another and less solitary excursion.

I went inland one day on an absurd railway to Notabile or Citta Vecchia, the old capital of the island. There I saw numerous ancient buildings, many of them of Norman construction, three churches, a cathedral containing a portrait of the Madonna painted by St Luke and a good della Robbia plaque, an infinitely boring Roman villa with a well-preserved tessellated pavement, a consumptives' hospital, the cave where St Paul stayed on his visit to Publius (though this would seem anything but a courteous lodging), and a catacomb full of very dilapidated Byzantine frescoes which the custodian described as Phoenician – a term used among Maltese archaeologists to describe any work earlier than the Norman occupation.

About this time I began making inquiries at the shipping offices for a berth from Malta in any direction, and was told that these could very rarely be guaranteed, particularly at the present season. Preference was always given to passengers booking a long passage. One just had to take one's chance. I was getting a little impatient with the proprietor of the Great Britain, who had, in the last two days, developed a habit of popping suddenly out of his office whenever I sat down to have a d ik, and saying, ''Ullo, 'ullo. And 'ow's that book getting along? Y ou don't seem to be seeing much of the island,' adding encouragingly: 'You couldn't see a 'alf of it, not if you was to spend a lifetime 'ere, you couldn't.' I became aware of a slight claustrophobic itch at the back of my mind, to which I am always liable on small islands, and in this mood one day, less than a week after my arrival, I leant over the Cavalier of St James, looking down into the Grand Harbour. Then I saw below, among the fishing-boats and cargo ships and nondescript official launches and lighters, a very radiant new arrival; a large white motor vessel, built like a yacht with broad, clean decks and a single yellow funnel. I took the funicular down to the Custom House and looked at her from the quay. She was the *Stella Polaris*, on her second cruise from the one I had abandoned at Port Said. As I stood there the motor launch left her side and ran up to the quay, the Norwegian cross fluttering at its stern. Three or four passengers landed, carrying cameras and sunshades. With them was the purser. I greeted him and asked where they were bound. He said for Constantinople, Athens, Venice, and the Dalmatian coast. Was there a spare berth? He said there was. The *Stella* was not due to sail until next afternoon, but within an hour I had made my adieux at the Great Britain, paid my drink account, tipped the kind and tireless servants, assured the proprietor that he should have my warmest commendations to the British public, and moved my luggage down to the harbour. That afternoon I unpacked, sent a vast pile of clothes to the laundry, folded and hung up my suits, set in order the mass of papers I had accumulated, notes, photographs, letters, guidebooks, circulars, sketches, caught and killed two fleas I had picked up in the Manderaggio, and went above, very contentedly, to renew my acquaintance with the deck bar steward.

SIX

On our way east we stopped for the day at Crete. The little harbour of Candia was too small for the *Stella*, so we anchored outside in the bay, well sheltered by the headland of Cape Paragia and the island of Dia. Inside the fortified breakwater, with its finely carved Venetian lion, lay a jumble of ramshackle shipping – a small fishing fleet, two or three coastal sailing-boats, and some incredibly dissolute tramp steamers which ply between Piraeus and the islands. A cargo of wine was being loaded into one of these, bottled in goat-skins. These were quite black and stretched taut and hard. A strong stench, part vinous, part goaty, rose from them. A slightly superior vintage was being rolled on in casks. The wine of Crete is lowly esteemed by connoisseurs.

The inhabitants, who had assembled to stare at us, were a good-looking race, particularly the old men, who had noble aquiline noses and great grey beards. They wore waistcoats covered with braid and rather greasy tassels, and coloured handkerchiefs round their heads; some of them had very tight corduroy trousers and others very loose blue ones of Turkish pattern. The young men seemed different in type, being stockier and swarthier, but as most of them were sailors, or seamen of some kind, I suppose it is probable that they were not Cretans at all. The women assumed that decent unobtrusiveness that usually survives for a generation or two after Moslem domination.

There is one main street in the town and a labyrinth of divergent alleys. There is the façade of a ruined Venetian palace, and a battered Venetian fountain carved with lions and dolphins. There is also a mosque, built up in places with capitals and fragments of carved stone work from other Venetian buildings. The top has been knocked off the minaret and the building has been turned into a cinematograph, where, by an odd coincidence, a film was being exhibited named *L'Ombre de Harem*. The shops sold, mostly, hunks of very yellow and grey meat, old Turkish watches, comic German picture-postcards, and brightly patterned lengths of printed cotton.

I accompanied a party of fellow passengers to the museum to admire the barbarities of Minoan culture. Except for one or two examples of animal sculpture, particularly a stone frieze of cattle and a substantially restored bull's head with fine sweeping horns, I saw nothing to suggest any genuine aesthetic feeling at all. It is interesting to notice how often a simplification and stylization of animal form is the intermediate stage between Art and Arts and Crafts. Young women in England who delight to make the nastiest kind of pot, will sometimes model very pretty lambs and calves.

It is less easy to come to a firm decision about the merits of Minoan painting, since only a few square inches of the vast area exposed to our consideration are earlier than the last twenty years, and it is impossible to disregard the suspicion that their painters have tempered their zeal for accurate reconstruction with a somewhat inappropriate predilection for covers of *Vogue*. Without some determined sacrifice of diffidence, some frank assertion of personal taste, it would have been impossible to cope at all with the problem of making a large, decorative composition out of the few discoloured fragments at the archaeologists' disposal. It is ungrateful to complain, but I do think that it is now harder, rather than less hard, to form any clear impression of Minoan painting.

We chartered a Ford car and drove with a guide to Cnossos, where Sir Arthur Evans (our guide referred to him always as 'Your English Lord Evans') is rebuilding the palace. At present only a few rooms and galleries are complete, the rest being an open hillside scarred with excavations, but we were able to form some idea of the magnitude and intricacy of the operation from the plans which were posted up for our benefit on the chief platform. I think that if our English Lord Evans ever finishes even a part of his vast undertaking, it will be a place of oppressive wickedness. I do not think that it can be only imagination and the recollection of a bloodthirsty mythology which makes something fearful and malignant of the cramped galleries and stunted alleys, these colonnades of inverted, conical pillars, these rooms that are mere blind passages at the end of sunless staircases; this squat little throne, set on a landing where the paths of the palace intersect; it is not the seat of a lawgiver nor a divan for the recreation of a soldier; here an ageing despot might crouch and have borne to him, along the walls of a whispering gallery, barely audible intimations of his own murder.

That afternoon I went for a walk alone, by the coast for a mile or so along a strip of railway-track to a quarry or cement works of some kind, then inland by the banks of a stream on a very English footpath lined with rankly growing wild flowers and thistles and bearded barley, and so back to the town, where I got lost in the environs and mocked by a troop of small children. There was one pretty incident of my visit which I only discovered later. I took a camera with me to Cnossos and left it in the car when we went over the excavations. I remember being mildly surprised later in the day, when I came to photograph the harbour, to see by the number that I had exposed more of the film than I thought. When it came back from the ship's photographic shop after being developed I was surprised to find a picture I had never taken; it was incorrectly focused and the perspective was crazily distorted by the angle at which the camera had been held. Nevertheless, it was recognizable as the Ford car in which we had driven to Cnossos, with the driver sitting very upright at the wheel. He must have induced one of his friends to take it while we were at the palace, and I thought it argued a nice nature in the man. He could not have hoped either to receive a print or even to see our surprise when the result of his little joke became visible. If he had merely wished to meddle with an unaccustomed piece of mechanism he would have left the film exposed at the same place, and so ruined both his own and my next photograph. I like to think that he wished to add a more durable bond to our relationship than the fleeting obligation of two hours' hire; he wanted to emphasize his individual existence as a separate thing from the innumerable, impersonal associations of the tourist. I am sure he was amused at the thought of the little surprise he had stored up for us, when we cursorily paid him his fare and went back to our ship. I expect he experienced something of the satisfaction which those eccentric (and regrettably rare) benefactors derive from sending banknotes anonymously to total strangers. If only his technical ability had come up to his good nature, I would have reproduced his portrait in this book, but I am afraid that, in the only form I possess, it would do him no further credit.

We spent the night at anchor and sailed early next morning so as to pass the Cyclades in daylight. The islands were beautiful, and all the passengers assembled on deck with telescopes and binoculars to watch their passage. One of them told me that on Santorini there still survives a Venetian colony, speaking a slightly debased sixteenth-century Italian. They are mostly the descendants of noble families; although sunk economically to the status of peasants they still live in the ruins of their palaces, with mouldering escutcheons over their doors – a whole town of Tesses of the D'Urbervilles – and have never intermarried with the Greeks, towards whom they exhibit an inherited superiority, little justified by their present condition.

We passed a new island, recently erupted from the sea – a heap of smoking volcanic matter, as yet quite devoid of life. Then past Naxos, Paros, and Mykonos into the Aegean, and so north to the Dardanelles, making fifteen knots through a calm sea. 'Can't you just see the quin-quē-remes?' said an American lady to me, as we leant on the rail, near each other. 'From distant Ophir,' she added, 'with a cargo of ivory, sandalwood, cedarwood, and sweet white wine.' I could not, but with a little more imagination I think I might easily have seen troopships, full of young Australians, going to their death with bare knees.

We were in the Hellespont when I awoke next morning, and passed Suvla Bay and Gallipoli before noon. The sea was pale green and opaque with the ice water that was coming down from the Black Sea. The Sea of Marmora was choppy; we ran under cold winds and a grey sky, broken by fitful bursts of sunlight. In the early afternoon we came in sight of Constantinople.

Owing to some confusion by the harbour authorities, we were unable immediately to obtain a berth on the Galata quay, so we employed the two hours' delay in cruising up the Bosphorus to the mouth of the Black Sea. It was too early in the year to see this at its best, but even on this cloudy and bleak afternoon the shore was attractive enough to keep us on deck in our overcoats. It seemed to me rather like the river banks of Devon, the Dart, for instance, or the estuary at Bideford, with their low green hills, covered with parkland and woods and dotted with villas and country houses.

We passed flight after flight of small birds, moving very fast and low just over the surface of the water, and uttering sad little cries.

I was told that they are peculiar to these waters. Little is known about their habits, where they build or where they come from; they are never seen to rest inland. It is reported, quite credibly it seemed to me, by the local fishermen that these are the souls of the Christian soldiers and sailors, Russian, Venetian, English, Australian, Greek, who in the centuries have fallen on Turkish soil, attempting to reconquer the great Christian capital from the Mohammedans. They fly backwards and forwards looking for Christian ground to rest on, always hoping that the vows they took may have been fulfilled by their successors.

It was getting dark by the time that we came back to the mouth of the Golden Horn. A low sea mist was hanging about the town, drifting and mingling with the smoke from the chimneys. The domes and towers stood out indistinctly, but even in their obscurity formed a tremendous prospect; just as the sun was on the horizon it broke through the clouds, and, in the most dramatic way possible, threw out a great splash of golden light over the minarets of St Sophia. At least, I think it was St Sophia. It is one of the delights of one's first arrival by sea at Constantinople to attempt to identify this great church from the photographs among which we have all been nurtured. As one approaches, dome after dome comes into view, and receives, each in its turn, little gasps of homage. Finally, when the whole immense perspective has been laid before us, two buildings contend for recognition. The more imposing one is the Mosque of Ahmed I. One can identify it by its distinction, unique except for the Kaaba at Mekka, of having six minarets. A more convincing way, however, of carrying one's point, is to say, 'That' – pointing wherever you choose – 'is Agia Sophia.'

'Agia' will always win the day for one. A more recondite snobbism is to say 'Aya Sophia', but except in a very sophisticated circle, who will probably not need guidance in the matter at all, this is liable to suspicion as a mere mispronunciation.

I spent the next day with a party of fellow passengers visiting the more obvious sights of the town – all of them far too famous to require description. It was an interesting example of the new regime in Turkey, that the dragoman assigned to us by the Natta tourist agency was a woman, a very plain, plump, self-possessed little person, who instructed us in a manner of maddening gentleness and forbearance, as though she were conducting a school treat of young children who had to be amused but kept well in hand. She had none of the flattery or invention of the male guide, and seemed to lack any genuine curiosity about the subjects she spoke of. Some sort of guide is necessary in Constantinople if one does not speak Turkish. She certainly piloted us quite successfully to a great number of interesting places in a short space of time. We saw Agia Sophia, a majestic shell full of vile Turkish fripperies, whose whole architectural rectitude has been fatally disturbed by the reorientation of the *mihrab*. We saw the famous blue mosque, where the effect of the fine blue-green tiles of the walls, mostly, I think, of Persian workmanship, is hurt by the crude Reckitt's blue of the painting and the characterless vulgarity of the patterns inside the dome. In Cairo I have noted the pride and superiority which a Western mind must feel when confronted with Arabic art; this feeling is intensified and broadened a hundred times in relation to everything Turkish. They seem to have been unable to touch any existing work or to imitate any existing movement without degrading it. It will be interesting to see, now that they have stumbled upon woman's suffrage and secularism, what their natural genius for vilification will make of those two essentially Western anomalies. We visited the great underground cistern, which is still the principal reservoir of the town, with its forest of marble columns. It is now lighted by electricity, and fails to give the same impression of illimitable extent which is recorded by those earlier travellers who rowed round it by torchlight. It is a fine, big cistern, however, and well worth seeing. We went to see a fort called Seven Towers. This, our guide informed us, was used for imprisoning 'Criminals, foreign ambassadors, and so forth'. We visited a military museum in a desecrated Christian basilica. It was like the hall of the worst kind of English country house, full of suits of armour, embroidered velvet banners and saddle-cloths, drums and trumpets, extravagantly ornamented fire-arms, and bayonets and daggers tastefully and ingeniously arranged in stars and rosettes and suns. We lunched at the Tokatlian, where the *hors d'oeuvres* were described on the menu as 'various tidbits'. Here the hall porter approached me in a fatherly manner, and, as we might offer a cigarette card or a postage stamp to a little boy, asked if I would like to have label of an hotel at Therapia to stick on my trunk. I was pleased to notice at the end of the cruise, when the luggage was stacked on the quay at Harwich, that many of my fellow passengers had been sympathetic to this suggestion. After luncheon we went to the Great Bazaar, which, owing largely to the edict forbidding Oriental clothes, is far less superficially exciting than the Mouski at Cairo. It is very much better, however, for actual shopping. I could not afford to buy anything myself, but I saw many delightful objects, eikons from Asia Minor, pretty eighteenth-century clocks and snuff boxes, Oriental embroideries, nineteenth-century colour prints, ingenious mechanical toys from the disbanded harems, etc., which others had bought at fairly reasonable prices.

After this, with only about two hours to spare, we went to the Serai, the palace of the Sultans, now converted into a public museum; the attendants are mostly the survivors of the royal eunuchs. One was a dwarf; he had a funny little shrivelled up, sexless face and a big black overcoat which brushed the ground and came very near to tripping him up once or twice. None of them were as big and fat as I had imagined. In the bad times before the secure establishment of the Kemalist regime, I am told that there was a big demonstration meeting held by the agitated eunuchs to protest against the abolition of polygamy; there was also about that time a procession of pimps demanding a higher percentage to cover the increased cost of living. Apparently the emancipation of women, there as elsewhere, had put a good deal of unfair amateur competition against the regular trade.

This may or may not be true. It did not seem to me my business to investigate statements of this kind, but simply to scribble them down in my notebook if they seemed to me amusing. But then, I have had three weeks in Fleet Street at one stage in my career. That is what people mean, I expect, when they say that newspaper training is valuable to an author.

The most striking thing about the Serai (regarded as a building and apart from the collections now exhibited there) is its astonishing discomfort. It somewhat resembles Earl's Court Exhibition, consisting, not of a single building, but of a large enclosed area, laid out roughly with lawns and trees, and strewn fortuitously with kiosks and pavilions of varying date and design. It is simply a glorified nomad encampment. Constantinople is by no means warm. The site was chosen for its political and geographical importance rather than for the serenity of its climate. Although on practically the same latitude as Naples, it is exposed to cold winds from the Steppes, and snow is not uncommon. Yet, in the five centuries of Turkish occupation, it seems never to have occurred to the sultans, with vast wealth and unlimited labour at their disposal, to provide any kind of covered corridor between the various rooms of their chief residence. Their highest aspirations towards physical luxury were confined to sprawling among gaudy silk cushions and munching sweetmeats while the icy wind whistled through the lattice-work over their heads. No wonder they took to drink. The treasures of the royal household, however, are staggering. Some idea of the economy of the Serai can be gained from the fact that the officials of the Kemalist party, when making a tour of the buildings in the first months of their occupation, came upon a room stacked from floor to ceiling with priceless sixteenth-century porcelain, still in the original contemporary wrappings in which it had arrived by caravan from China. It had been no one's business to unpack it, and there it had lain through the centuries. Theft and embezzlement must have been continuous and unchecked in the household. The astonishing thing is the amount of treasure that has survived the years of imperial bankruptcy. There are huge uncut emeralds and diamonds, great shapeless drops full of flaws, like half-sucked sweets; there is a gold throne set with cabuchons of precious stone; a throne of inlaid mother-o'-pearl and tortoiseshell; there are cases of jewelled pipe mouthpieces, and of dagger-hilts, watches, cigar-holders, snuff boxes, hand-mirrors, brushes, combs – twenty or thirty of each, all supremely magnificent; there is a dressing-table presented by Catherine the Great, encrusted all over, every inch of it, with rose-coloured paste jewels; there is a dressing-table presented by Frederick the Great, covered with alabaster and amber; there is an exquisite Japanese garden and temple made of filigree gold and enamel; there is a model paddle steamer, made of red and white gold with diamond port-holes and ruby and emerald pennons; there is the right hand and the skull of St John the Baptist; there are jewels to be worn in turbans and jewels to be worn round the neck on chains and jewels to be worn by women and jewels to be played with and tumbled listlessly between the fingers from hand to hand. They are not, of course, of equal quality; even to my most inexpert eye it was clear that many of the stones, most impressive by their bulk, would emerge quite inconsiderable from the hands of a modern stone-cutter. Even so, their value, if they are genuine, should be enough to rescue any budget. The guide made a round estimate of each object in turn as being worth 'more than a million dollars'. One cannot help doubting, however, whether, in the prolonged period of Turkish insolvency, some depredations were not made upon this hoard. It would have been so easy to prize out a cabuchon emerald or so with the fingernail and replace it with a jujube, that I feel it must have been done from time to time – who knows how often?

Immediately in front of me in our tour of inspection there travelled a very stout, rich lady from America, some of whose conversation I was privileged to overhear. Whatever the guide showed her, china, gold, ivory, diamond or amber, silk or carpet, this fortunate lady was able casually to remark that she had one like that at home. '*Why*,' she would say, 'whoever would have thought that *that* was of any value. I've got three like that, that Cousin Sophy left me, bigger, of course, but just the same pattern, put away in one of the store-rooms. I must have them out when I get back. I never looked on *them* as being anything much.'

But she had to admit herself beaten by the right hand and skull of St John the Baptist.

During this visit I did not bother at all about the classical antiquities, but returned to the Serai again next day for a prolonged inspection. I also had my hair cut in a very up-to-date shop in Pera, opposite the Tokatlian. It had a front in the latest Parisian taste that might have been designed by M. Lalique himself, and a window full of the bottles of Guerlain and Chanel, and complete outfits of Elizabeth Arden. Inside there were rows of marble basins with numerous silver taps; there were silver ovens for heating towels; electric cables and switches for every kind of friction and ultra-violet ray; there were chairs like operating tables which could be tilted to any angle by pressure of the foot; the brushes, the moment they were used, were dropped into a chute like cards at a Casino, from which they emerged later sterilized and sealed up in air-proof paper wrappings. There were hairdressers in white overalls, and manicurists trotting about with little stools and boxes of instruments. Yet I am sorry to say that with all these attractions the place smelled very strongly of drains, the water from the hot spray was tepid and discoloured, and the electrical machines emitted long blue sparks, crackled, and did no more.

I lunched at the Embassy, a fine, stately building constructed in the last century on the model, so I was told, of the Reform Club in London, and soon to be reluctantly abandoned for the desolation of Angora. Osbert and Sacheverel Sitwell were there, combining a gay enthusiasm for the subtleties of Turkish rococo with unfathomable erudition about Byzantine archaeology and the scandals of Ottoman diplomacy. Back to the Serai after luncheon, and then to the *Stella*. We sailed that afternoon just before sunset.

The chief subject of conversation on board that evening was an accident which had occurred in the harbour. The ferry steamer which travels between Galata and Scutari, on the other side of the Bosphorus, had run on to the rocks in the morning mist; the passengers had been removed without loss of life but only just in time. There was a newcomer in the *Stella* – a very elegant Greek who wore an Old Etonian tie and exhibited an extensive acquaintance with the more accessible members of the English peerage. He had been on board the ferry boat at the time of the disaster, and he gave a very interesting account of his experience. The ship had been crowded with labourers going across to their work. At the first impact the Captain and his chief officer leaped into the only boat and made off. Later in the day the Captain resigned his command, on the grounds that this was the third time it had happened in eighteen months and his nerves were not what they had been. Left to themselves the passengers, who were a motley race of Turks, Jews, and Armenians, fell into a state of mad panic. The only helpful course would have been to sit absolutely firm and hope for rescue. Instead they trotted moaning from side to side, swaying the ship to and fro and shaking it off the rocks on which it was impaled. My informant sat, frozen with terror, on one of the seats, in expectation of almost immediate capsize. He was here met by a stout little man, strutting calmly along the deck with a pipe in his mouth and his hands plunged into the pockets of his ulster. They observed each other with mutual esteem as the frenzied workmen jostled and shouted round them.

'I perceive, sir,' said the man with the pipe, 'that you, too, are an Englishman.'

'No,' answered the Greek, 'only a damned foreigner.'

'I beg your pardon, sir,' said the Englishman, and walked to the side of the ship, to drown alone.

Fortunately, however, there was no drowning. Boats came out from the shore and removed all the passengers before the ship foundered.

The Greek was travelling only as far as Athens. I spent most of next day in his company. He asked me searching questions about 'aestheticism' at Oxford. He had been at the House, but remarked with a shade of regret that he had not found any 'aestheticism' in his day. Was it because of 'aestheticism' that Oxford did so badly at athletics. I said, no, the evil was deeper than that. I didn't mind telling another Oxford man, but the truth was, that there was a terrible outbreak of drug-taking at the University.

'Cocaine?'

'Cocaine,' I said, 'and worse.'

'But do the dons do nothing to stop it?'

'My dear man, the dons are the origin of the whole trouble.'

He said that there had been practically no drug-taking at the House in his time.

He renewed the attack later in the day. Would I come down to his cabin to have a drink?

I said I would have a drink with him by all means, but in the deck bar.

He said, 'I can see you are Scottish because of your blue eyes. I had a very dear friend who was a Scotchman. You remind me a little of him.'

Later, he said, would I come to his cabin to look at a silver Turkish inkpot. I said no, but I would love to see it on deck. It was very ugly.

When he disembarked he invited me to luncheon at the Grande Bretagne. I said, yes, but next day he did not turn up.

We arrived just before dinner and moored in Phaleron Bay. That evening there was a fancy-dress ball on board. Some of the passengers had brought very elaborate costumes with them, others hired simple ones from the ship's barber; others contented themselves with a false nose or a mask, but everyone did something, even the oldest.

Prizes were awarded for the best dresses. After the band had gone to bed various groups split up and disappeared with bottles of champagne to continue the party in their cabins. The purser was in very good form that evening – a man of rare social gifts and unflagging spirit.

I had been to Athens once before, at a time when I had never been farther from England than Paris. I shall not easily forget the romance of my first arrival. I came from Marseilles in the *Patris II*, a Hellenic national ship of fairly recent construction. It was in winter and we had rough weather most of the way. I shared a cabin with a Greek currant merchant who did not move from his bed during the five days' voyage. The only other English-speaking first-class passenger was a blustering American engineer. I sat on deck most of the time, feeling rather ill and reading James's *Varieties of Religious Experience*. At intervals the American and I drank *mastika*. He said if one ever drank *mastika* one returned to Greece; sometimes I went and looked over at the 'deck passengers', huddled under improvised tents, scratching their feet, and always eating. Piraeus was our first stop. Sun had set and the harbour was all alight when we came in. There was a long delay before we could land. The rowing boats came out all round us packed so tight that one could have walked ashore, all the boatmen shouting for custom. The friends I was visiting had come out to meet me, and sat bobbing below and shouting up, 'Evelyn.' They had brought their valet with them to deal with the luggage – a man of singular ferocity who had been a hired assassin at Constantinople under the old regime. He and the boatmen took up the cry 'EE-lin! EE-lin!'

Then my luggage got into the hands of the wrong boatman, and he and that valet had a fight which the valet won very easily by means of an outrageous but wholly conclusive foul blow. Then we went ashore and drove very quickly from Piraeus to Athens, along a road cleft and scarred as if by bombardment, in a very ramshackle Morris car which had no lamps or brakes or hooter, but was freed from police molestation by a diplomatic number and a little Union Jack between the places where the headlights ought to have been.

It was the Orthodox Christmas Day, and the streets were full of people shaking hands and kissing and letting off fireworks in each other's eyes. We went straight to a night club kept by a one-legged

Maltese, who gave us cocktails made out of odd drugs and a spirit of his own distilling.

Later the *première danseuse* of the cabaret came out and sat at our table and warned us on no account to touch the cocktails. It was too late.

Later still I drove round the city in a taxi-cab on I forget what errand, and then back to the night club. The taxi-driver followed me to our table. I had given him as a tip over ten pounds in drachmas, my watch, my gloves, and my spectacle-case. It was too much, he protested.

The rest of my visit was rather overshadowed by this introduction to Athenian life. In fact, it was not until I had been very seasick on the way home that I fully recovered from the effects of that evening. That was in my undergraduate days, and it makes me feel unnaturally old to recall them.

But even now, in comparative maturity, my second visit to Athens coincided with my introduction to a new sort of drink. As soon as I landed I took a taxi into the town, to visit a friend called Alastair who lived at this time in a little house in the eastern quarter, under the slopes of Lycabettus, in a side street off the Kolonaki Square. This house was full of mechanical singing birds and eikons, one of which, oddly enough the most modern, had miraculous powers. One of Alastair's servants gave notice, on the grounds that it used to stretch an arm out of the picture and bang him over the head when he neglected his work. Alastair was not yet dressed. I told him that I had had a late night, drinking after the ball with some charming Norwegians, and felt a little shaken. He then made me this drink, which I commend to anyone in need of a wholesome and easily accessible pick-me-up. He took a large tablet of beet sugar (an equivalent quantity of ordinary lump sugar does equally well) and soaked it in Angostura Bitters and then rolled it in Cayenne pepper. This he put into a large glass which he filled up with champagne. The excellences of this drink defy description. The sugar and Angostura enrich the wine and take away that slight acidity which renders even the best champagne slightly repugnant in the early morning. Each bubble as it rises to the surface carries with it a red grain of pepper, so that as one drinks one's appetite is at once stimulated and gratified, heat and cold, fire and liquid, contending on one's palate

123

and alternating in the mastery of one's sensations. I sipped this almost unendurably desirable drink and played with the artificial birds and musical boxes until Alastair was ready to come out. I had another friend in Athens called Mark, and with these two I spent two very delightful days, sleeping in Alastair's house and rejoining the *Stella* just before she sailed. I did not revisit the Tower of Winds or the Temple of Theseus or the Acropolis, and will say nothing about them here, except to remark about the last that it is not 'snow-white', as I have seen it described by quite responsible observers, but a singularly beautiful tone of very pale pinkish brown; the nearest parallel to it in Nature that I can think of is that of the milder parts of a Stilton cheese into which port has been poured. We did, however, after lunching at the Grande Bretagne, drive out to the church at Daphne. I think I should be trespassing too dangerously upon Mr Robert Byron's ground if I were to venture upon any eulogy of these superb mosaics. They have had a disturbed history, what with the arrows of the Crusaders – who were moved by the theological differences of the Western and Eastern patriarchates to shoot away the eyes from the vast head of Christ in the dome – the Turks, who lit log fires in the nave, and, in quite recent times, the missiles of lunatics, who used to resort there from a neighbouring institution, and employed the time between their devotions in throwing stones and old bottles at the glittering ceiling; large parts of them, however, have survived intact and constitute one of the finest existing monuments of Byzantine art.

From Daphne we drove along the Eleusis road, pursued at times by savage sheep-dogs, and then turned off by the cart road below Mount Aegaleos to an isolated café overlooking the bay of Salamis. It was Sunday afternoon, and there were several other parties sitting under the Hawaian thatched arbour. There was a photographer making little tin-type photographs which, when developed, usually revealed his own thumb print and little else. There were two students, male and female, in football shorts and open shirts, with rugged staffs and haversacks. There was a very happy family of Athenian bourgeoises. They had a baby with them. This they first sat on the table, then on the top of their car; then they put it upside down on a chair; then it was put astride a clothes line and rocked gently backwards and forwards, then it was put into the bucket of the well and let down out of sight, then it was given a bottle of gaseous lemonade, a more perilous drink in Athens than in any town in the world. To all these efforts towards its entertainment it responded with chirrups of happy laughter and big, frothy bubbles dribbling down its chin. There was also a limousine containing two very *mondaine* young ladies, who would not come into the open, but sat back hardly visible among cut velvet upholsteries and were waited upon by two adolescent military officers; now and then the window would be let down and jewelled fingers would appear, haughtily discarding a sheet of silver paper or a banana skin.

Mark and Alastair and I sat in the shade and drank a carafe of resinated white wine and ate Turkish delight, while the photographer capered before us with his camera and caused us to purchase enough copies of his thumb print to convict him of any crime in the Greek statute book.

We went back to the *Stella* for dinner and then returned to see the night life. First we went to an underground café decorated with pseudo-Russian frescoes. Here we saw most of the English colony, engaged in those fervent intrigues, part social, part political, part personal, which embellish and enrich Athenian life more than that of any capital in Europe. But the entertainment was confined to one pianist in Georgian peasant dress. We asked if there was to be no cabaret. 'Alas,' said the manageress. 'Not tonight. Last night there was a German gentleman here, and he bit the girls so terribly in the legs that tonight they say they will not dance!'

From there we went to the Folies Bergères, which was very chic and Parisian; the waiter tried to induce us to order champagne, and a Hungarian Jewess performed Oriental dances in a Chu-Chin-Chow slave market costume, modestly supplemented with pink cotton tights. Mark's boredom soon became uncontrollable, so we called for our bill, paid them half what they demanded (which they accepted with every manifestation of gratitude), and left.

We walked across the gardens to the poorer part of the town. Of the many smells of Athens two seem to me the most characteristic – that of garlic, bold and deadly like acetylene gas, and that of dust, soft and warm and caressing like tweed. It was in this dusty smell that we walked in the garden, but garlic met us at the bottom of the steps

which led from the street to the door of the ΜΠΑΡ[1] ΘΕΛΛΑΤΟΕ;
it was garlic sweetened, however, by the savour of roast lamb. There
were two lambs impaled horizontally on spits, sizzling over an open
charcoal fire. The atmosphere was one of Dickensian conviviality.
Only men were present, most of them peasants come up from the
country for the night. They all smiled greetings to us, and one of
them sent three mugs of beer across to our table. This began a
tremendous round of ceremonious health-drinking which was still
going on by the time we left. It is the commendable practice of the
Greeks never to serve drink without food, usually a little bit of garlic
sausage, or bad ham on the end of a match; these appear in little
saucers, and our table was soon strewn with them.

Two men in the corner were playing guitars of a kind, and others
were dancing, with very severe expressions on their faces but a
complete lack of self-consciousness. They were Pyrrhic dances of
indefinable antiquity. Four of them danced together, going through
the various figures with great solemnity. If one of them made a false
move it was as though he had dropped a catch in an English cricket
match; they accepted his apologies in as sporting a spirit as they
could assume, but it clearly was a grave wrong, not lightly to be
dismissed or expiated except by prodigies of accuracy in the future.
Moreover, as in cricket, the amateur status was jealously preserved.
So far from taking a hat round after the performance, the dancers
themselves paid a few halfpence to the band. There was keen competition to dance, the fours being already made up and eagerly
waiting for their turn to take the floor. The only fight which occurred
that evening was occasioned by one rather tipsy young man attempting to perform out of his turn. They all set on him and pummelled
him for his bad manners, but later it was made up and they drank
his health. I had not since I left England, and seldom before that,
found myself in a company so lacking in avarice. No one made the
smallest attempt to get anything out of us, but, on the contrary,
repeatedly offered us beer and cigarettes and would take nothing
except as an exchange of courtesy. Alastair reminded me of how we
had once gone into a small pub in a fishing village in North Devon.

1. There is no B sound in the modern Greek, B being pronounced like V. One of
the simpler delights of Greek is one's continual discovery of English words in Greek
characters. Cinema has come back to them after a long journey spelled with a Σ.

Five or six fishermen were sitting round the parlour sipping half-pints of cider. We ordered ourselves a half-pint each and asked the landlord to provide a round of drinks. When we asked for the reckoning he told us twelve shillings. They had each asked for a treble whisky. We did not think any the worse of them. Except during the salmon season they could never afford spirits. We were clearly rich to them. Still, the atmosphere at the Thellatos was different.

As the evening went on the conversation became more animated. I was, of course, quite unable to follow it, but Alastair said it was mostly about politics; an uninstructed discussion but full of high feeling. There was an elderly man with a curly grey beard who was much moved. He roared and pounded on the table with his fist; he pounded on his glass, broke it, and cut himself. He stopped arguing and began to cry. Immediately everyone else stopped arguing too and came over to comfort him. They wrapped a grubby handkerchief round his hand, which was not, I think, at all seriously injured. They gave him beer and bits of bad ham on matches; they patted him on the back and put their arms round his neck and kissed him. Soon he was smiling again and the discussion was resumed, but as soon as he showed signs of excitement, they warned him with smiles, by moving his mug farther across the table.

At last, after a great many adieux, we climbed up the steps again into the fresh air, and so home under the orange-trees through the warm darkness that smelled like tweed.

Next morning Alastair had to go to the Chancery to decode telegrams, so Mark and I went shopping in Shoe Lane – the street in the old Turkish quarter where all the second-hand dealers have their stalls. Mark continued some negotiations which, he told me, had already been protracted for three weeks, concerning the purchase of a grotto constructed by Anatolian refugees out of cork and looking-glass and pieces of sponge; only the price prevented me from buying a marble statuette of an association footballer.

The *Stella* was sailing at noon for Venice, and I narrowly escaped missing the last launch from the shore, Mark delaying me by the gift of three religious postcards, a balloon, and a basket of black olives.

Immediately after luncheon we passed through the Corinth canal, which, for some reason I could not understand, attracted many of the passengers more than anything they had yet seen on their travels.

It took some time to go through, but they remained on deck, photographing it and talking about it and making water-colour sketches of its featureless stone sides, while I went to my cabin and dozed; I had a good deal of sleep to make up and this seemed an opportunity.

We reached Corfu early next morning and spent the day there. It is a long, thin, hilly island separated from the mainland by a narrow channel, just opposite the Greek–Albanian border. It has one fair-sized, comparatively wealthy town, a mountain of 3,000 feet, and two lakes. In classical times it was called Kerkyra; Odysseus was shipwrecked here and met Nausicaa by a little brook on the south-west side of the island. Later it belonged to the Venetians, who built the now dilapidated fortifications of the harbour; in the nineteenth century the English held it and built the admirable roads which distinguish it from the other Greek islands; thanks to the scarcity of wheeled traffic these are still in excellent repair. It now belongs to the Greeks, who have attempted to revert to its earlier name, so that 'Kerkyra' is now carved by the convicts on the olive-wood animals which are hawked everywhere in the streets. I do not know whether this paragraph of rather rudimentary information may seem an impertinence. I can only assume in my reader the same ignorance that I had myself when I first went there.

Frankly I had never heard of the place when, after my first visit to Greece, I stopped there for a few hours in a vile ship called the *Yperoke*, where I was travelling second class in barely conceivable discomfort. It seemed to me then one of the most beautiful places I had ever seen. So much was I impressed, that when, later, I found myself writing a novel about someone very rich, I gave her a villa in Corfu, as I thought that, when I was rich, that was one of the first things I would buy. I still think so, and if enough people buy this book I shall fulfil my intention. It is full of lovely villas, many of them for sale. Before the war the harbour was much frequented by private yachts, and during the season the shores were peopled by a very gay cosmopolitan society. It has become less fashionable since the collapse of the Central Powers, but all the more habitable. Do let me urge you, gentle reader, if you have only borrowed this book from a library, to buy two or three copies instantly so that I can leave London and go and live peacefully on this island.

The chief merchandise of the island seemed to be live tortoises and the olive-wood animals I have mentioned, as made by the convicts in the prison. Several passengers in the *Stella* bought tortoises, few of which survived the voyage; tortoise races became an added attraction to the deck games. The chief disability suffered by tortoises as racing animals is not their slowness so much as their confused sense of direction. I had exactly the same difficulty when I used to take part in sports at my school, and was repeatedly disqualified for fouling the other competitors.

There are, as far as I know – and Baedeker by his silence seems to confirm this – no antiquities or sites of historic interest in Corfu. There are walks and drives among the natural beauties of the hills and streams and sea-coast and lake, and the artificial beauties of rich little farms, slightly disorderly in their exuberant fertility. There is a town sparkling with unembarrassed, provincial sociability, cafés, concert halls, a theatre, a good hotel, arcaded streets of shops, the seat of two archbishops, Latin and Orthodox, a casino, a garrison of soldiers, innumerable sailors of all nationalities, a harbour full of shipping. There is a temperate and endearing climate. I cannot conceive why rich people go and live on the French Riviera when there are places like Corfu left in the world.

I did not do very much during our day there, as, indeed, there is very little to do. I pottered round the town and harbour renewing my feelings of envy and aspiration. After luncheon I drove in a horse-carriage along the Vide Imperatore Guglielmo, which is bordered by groves of olive, rose, and orange-trees, to the little balustraded platform called, in the old style, Canone Point, or, in its Hellenized version, ΣΤΟΗ ΚΑΝΟΝΙ. This is the extreme point of the peninsula that runs out from the town, enclosing the fiord called Lake Kaliki-copulo. There used to be a battery here of one gun. Now there is a café-restaurant. The bank falls steeply down to the water, where there are two tiny islands, the one wooded, containing a villa that was once, I think, a monastery; the other is very small and is completely occupied by a minute chapel, two cypress-trees, and a parsonage. It is accessible from the beach by stepping-stones. I went down to it. There were two little bells in the tower, and, inside, some quite black eikons and a hen laying an egg. The priest appeared magically, rowing a boat full of vegetables from the opposite bank.

His son sat in the stern with bare legs crossed under him, nursing a tin of Californian peaches. I gave some money to the church expenses and climbed up the hill path to the café. One or two other passengers had arrived from the *Stella*. I joined them, and ate sponge fingers and drank some delicious Corfiote wine, that looks like the juice of blood oranges and tastes like cider and costs, or should cost when one is not obviously a tourist, about twopence. A band appeared, of two guitars and a fiddle. The fiddler was quite young but blind. They played, 'Yes, sir, That's my Baby,' in the oddest way conceivable, and laughed aloud with pleasure at the money they collected.

In my very brief visit I became more attached to Corfu than any place I can think of. I was sorry to leave, but I think that there, more than anywhere, I felt the disadvantage of arriving on a pleasure ship. At Venice I was quite unconscious of any such feeling. The moment she was anchored in the mouth of the Grand Canal, the *Stella* simply became an unusually comfortable hotel. We spent two days there and then sailed for Ragusa.

What can I possibly write, now, at this stage of the world's culture, about two days in Venice, that would not be an impertinence to every educated reader of this book? Am I to say that it consists of an archipelago of one hundred and thirty-five islands transected by a hundred and forty-five canals; that on one of these islands stands a church, dedicated to St Mark, filled with mosaics of peculiar splendour; that on another of these islands there is a disused sailors' hostel, called the Scuola San Rocco, with frescoes on its walls and ceiling by Jacopo Tintoretto (1512–1594); that the Venetians were once a virtuous and a very wealthy race who had 'learned Christianity from the Greeks, chivalry from the Normans, and the laws of human life and toil from the ocean itself'; that nowadays they are less virtuous and less wealthy, and subsist, in fact, entirely upon the foreigners who come to admire the works of their forefathers? Or shall I say that I ate *scampi* at Cavaletto and felt no ill-effects; that I went to a prettily decorated rococo night club, called Luna, which had been a gambling-room in the time of Goldoni; that a lady I was with had a gold cigarette case stolen from her by a gondolier; that I met Berta Ruck in the Piazzetta and later Adrian Stokes, and walked with him in the rain over innumerable little bridges to visit places of interest that happened always to be shut;

how when the rain became intolerable we took refuge in a black-
smith's shop next door to a Palladian church, and when Adrian
asked the youth in charge of the shop what time the church opened,
he replied scornfully, how was he to know, he was in the next parish;
how the same youth asked whether the canals in London had been
frozen over that winter; how I went back with Adrian to tea in a very
grand apartment on the Giudecca full of Titians and Tiepolos, and
Adrian told me that Ruskin was all wrong about the dates of some
of the buildings he most admired; how for a long time I could not
think what it was that made the life of Venice seem so different from
any other town, until I realized that there was no traffic, and that
half the children of the town had never seen any horses except the
bronze ones outside St Mark's, and Adrian told me that when, some
months ago, a motor car had been landed on its way to the Lido,
the crowd was so great to see it that two people were pushed over
into the water and nearly drowned; how I discovered that an
acquaintance of mine was a legendary figure in Venice, well thought
of among the poor as the eccentric English milord who had bought
up all the cauliflowers in the vegetable market and floated them
down the Grand Canal; how I purchased a Tauchnitz edition of *St
Mark's Rest* at Alinari's, and reflected that unlike most men of letters,
Ruskin would have led a much more valuable life if he had been a
Roman Catholic?

No, it seems to me a moment for humility. Perhaps if I made my
home in Venice for twenty years and attained a perfect command
of medieval Italian; if I spent months in public and private libraries
translating and collating original sources; if I learned almost everything about the chemistry of painting, scraped bits off frescoes and
had them analysed, made X-ray studies of them, and trotted all over
Europe comparing them with other versions; if I steeped myself in
the latest aesthetic theories; if I became adept at particularizing
among all manner of conflicting and incongruous influences, tracing
in one and the same object, here the Byzantine, there the Moorish,
there the Catholic, Frankish, or Norman motive; if I became a
master of the subtle art of attribution, able delicately to shift reputation from shoulder to shoulder and identify the technique of one
anonymous mason from the baser imitations of another – then
perhaps I might decently contribute a chapter here to what has

already been written by those who have mastered all these accomplishments. Meanwhile, since there seems no probability of my ever becoming anything more considerable than one of a hundred globe-trotting novelists, I will pass on to Ragusa.

I think I may, without offence, assume in many of my readers an incomplete acquaintance with this town. It is now called Dubrovnik, a somewhat unhelpful change, after the manner of new nationalities, which coincided with the rechristening of Cattaro, Kotor and Spalato, Split. It has until quite lately had an interesting and honourable history, being one of the free city states of the west which, generation after generation, by courage and guile and good fortune, was enabled to maintain its integrity against barbarian influence. It was founded originally by the fugitives driven by heathen invasion from Salona and Epidamus; these established an aristrocratic administration of forty-five senatorial families and an elected rector, more or less parallel to the Council and Doge at Venice. They owed nominal allegiance to the Emperor at Byzantium until the Fourth Crusade, and after that to Venice, but they were in all practical matters self-governing and independent. They became wealthy through general trade and the salt mines at Stagno, and at the middle of the seventeenth century had a population of 33,000, with 360 vessels and a standing army of 4,000. They were obliged to live throughout the whole of this period in a state of perpetual defence, first against the Slavs, Bosnians, and Serbs, and later against the Turks, who became masters of the entire mainland, hemming them in precariously between the mountains and the sea. In 1667 Ragusa suffered a plague and earthquake which reduced it, in one catastrophe, from a thriving city to a small coast town. It recovered slowly and incompletely, and at the end of the eighteenth century passed into the hands of the Austrians, but, although no longer politically considerable, it remained Catholic, aristocratic, and cultured, immeasurably aloof from its savage neighbours. It was the simple task of the allied statesmen of the Peace Conference to undo the work of a thousand years and hand it over to its traditional enemies, the mongrel kingdom of the Jugo-Slavs.

There is a little harbour under the walls of Ragusa, but larger ships anchor off Gravosa, the commercial landing-stage a short tram-ride from the town. The day of our visit was a religious festival of the Eastern calendar, and the shops were therefore compulsorily closed. This was a real hardship on the inhabitants, to whom the arrival of a big ship is a rare and exceedingly lucrative occurrence; the overwhelming majority of them, all, in fact, except the Serbian officials and garrison, are Roman Catholics, for whom the day had no significance. The Slav officials, however, who, I think, are made to feel very conscious of their social inferiority in these imperial towns, were closely on the lookout for any infringement of the law, and it was only with difficulty that we could obtain access to the public buildings.

The chief of these are the Rector's Palace and the Sponza, or Custom House. These are naturally quite small and, after Venice, comparatively simple, but they are well preserved, dignified and peculiarly charming in design, and full of fine workmanship. The Rector's Palace is attributed to Michelozzo Michelozzi, the architect of the Palazzo Riccardi at Florence. The Custom House has a window and balcony of graceful fourteenth-century Venetian Gothic. There are also small Dominican and Franciscan monasteries, the latter containing an exquisite little romanesque cloister, planted in the centre with a garden of orange-trees, cactuses, and evergreens from which rise a little fountain and the statue of a saint. The churches, except for the crude and modern Orthodox cathedral, are all interesting; Santa Maria Maggiore contains two very dubious paintings attributed to Titian and Andrea del Sarto; San Salvatore has a lovely sixteenth-century façade; the cathedral is good early eighteenth-century baroque. There are remains of several of the noble houses, with armorial carvings over the doors, but most of these have sunk into poor hands and are split up into tenement dwellings; that the aristocratic tradition survived, however, was clear from the bearing of several very dowdy and very august grandes dames whom I observed at their prayers, and from the general courtesy and dignity of the townspeople. Most of these were smartly dressed and vivacious in manner, exchanging greetings and jokes at the cafés and promenading the broad main street of the town – called, inevitably, the Stradone – with a delightfully modified swagger. There were a few country people in from the hills, looking very clean and starched in their peasant costumes, the men with highly decorative daggers sticking from their sashes. There was a band playing in the evening in the main square outside the walls, and down in Gravosa they let off some fireworks, but whether in honour of the *Stella*'s arrival or of the Orthodox festival I was unable to discover. That evening we sailed down the coast to Cattaro.

Cattaro has been exposed to much the same historical influences as Ragusa, though her history is less eminent. She was never a free town except for thirty years at the beginning of the fifteenth century. Before that time she was held from 1185 successively by the Nemanja dynasty of Serbs, Lewis the Great of the Hungarian-Croat Empire, and the Bosnian King Tvrtko I. In 1420 she came again under Western influence, and was held by Venice until 1797, when the Austrians took possession of her, and, except for a brief interlude during the Napoleonic period when Russia and France had her in turn, remained in possession until the Peace Conference. The original Roman population became extensively diluted by Slav blood during the Middle Ages, but it is interesting to note, in view of modern Slavonic pretensions, that when the Venetians took over the town, Western culture had so far survived that all documents were still in Latin, and Italian was the language of the courts of law. From 1420 until 1918 the town was wholly under Western influence, until, with Ragusa and the rest of the Dalmatian coast, it was bundled into Jugo-Slavia.

Like Ragusa, it suffered from earthquakes and plagues, and has never recovered its medieval population. It is a smaller town than Ragusa, much less attractive architecturally, built on a triangle of alluvial soil at the end of a deep fiord. Owing to the strict limit imposed on expansion by the nature of the site, the streets are extremely narrow and the houses jumbled on top of each other; there is none of the spaciousness of Ragusa, and no equivalent to the Stradone; the people seemed poorer, less leisurely, less sociable with each other, less courteous to strangers; they stared and begged when we came ashore as they had not done at Ragusa. Nevertheless, it looked very attractive from the water, huddled at the foot of a great rock cleft away from the wooded hillside. A fortified stone wall climbed up this crag, protecting the town from the rear and making a triangle, with the sea front for base and the Citadel of St John as the apex, 260 metres up. Halfway up to the summit is a little chapel clearly visible from below.

Cattaro is full of churches – there are said to have been thirty at one time – all of them Roman Catholic except two; one of these is the repulsive modern Serbian-Orthodox cathedral of St Nicholas, and the other the fine twelfth-century church of St Lucas, which the Catholics handed over to Orthodox refugees from Turkish persecution in the middle of the seventeenth century. The largest and oldest Catholic church is St Tryphon's, but it has little to commend it except antiquity. St Tryphon is little known outside the town of his burial; his most renowned exploit was the cure of a widow's son who had been bitten by a basilisk, an incident which is attractively recorded in the fourteenth-century ciborium of the high altar. St Joseph's has a picture they claim is by Veronese, and St Mary's a crucifix of wood, plaster, and canvas attributed to Michelangelo; the Franciscan Church of St Clara has a very gorgeous baroque altar of coloured marble. The secular buildings are picturesque but boring. I do not think it is a town where anyone except the most hardened water-colourist would want to stay for very long.

There is a very good road built by the Austrians that leads up from Cattaro to Cetinje, the capital of Montenegro. On the atlas the distance looks very small, but the ascent is so steep that there are between twenty and thirty hairpin bends before it reaches the pass in the mountains and leads down to the plateau on which Cetinje stands. From the *Stella*'s deck one could trace the path up the mountain-side, twisting backwards and forwards among the rocks and scrub until it was lost to sight three thousand feet up. I joined the *Stella* expedition, and it took us two and a half hours' hard driving to cover the distance, which, as the crow flies, measured on the map, is rather under eight miles.

We started soon after breakfast in five or six cars, and arrived just at luncheon time. To avoid running in each other's dust, the drivers, as soon as we started, spaced themselves out at long intervals along the road. The ascent in places was so steep, and the road so carefully graded that we could shout to the parties above and below, although there was, perhaps, a half-mile of road between us, as though to someone in the upper windows of a house. By the time we reached the summit the *Stella* and the fiord in which she lay had grown minute and unreal, and a great stretch of the Adriatic coast lay exposed behind us, and in front and on either side ridge upon ridge of mountain.

The road ran straight for some distance; the air was cold and clear; there were patches and drifts of snow in sheltered places and no sign of human habitation. No sign of human habitation, but many signs of human activity. I have but a very slight acquaintance with mountainous country, so I cannot tell whether I am recording a commonplace of all such districts or whether what surprised me so much was indeed peculiar to Montenegro. That was that the boulders and cliffs that comprised the landscape all round us were varied at quite frequent intervals by deep, usually circular craters and basins, with rocky sides and a flat surface of soil at the bottom, no bigger in many cases than the floor of a large room, at the most not thirty yards in diameter. Yet in the majority of cases these little pot-holes of earth, so inaccessible from farm or market, bore every indication of being rudely but carefully cultivated. The crop, whatever it was, was still quite immature, just regular lines of green shoots protruding a few inches above the soil, but it was quite clearly no accidental growth. It puzzled me very much to think who could be the farmer of these ungrateful acres.

Presently the road began to descend slightly, and then ran quite straight across a plain of arable land into Cetinje. Since it is the capital of a large province, and was until quite recently the capital of an independent kingdom, it is seemly to speak of Cetinje as a town, though actually it is no more than a large village, spaciously laid out and ornamented by one or two public buildings, no larger certainly than might be found in most English villages, but in this part of the world uncommonly large for anything except a town of some importance. The palace is about the size of the average English rectory; its largest room is occupied by a billiard table, which so far eclipsed the other concomitants of royalty in the eyes of the neighbouring highlanders that the palace became known, not as the house of the king, but as Billjarda, the house of the billiard table. This billiard table added very considerably to the prestige of the royal family, but it had the disadvantage of entirely filling the only room suitable for official receptions. These, indeed, occurred so rarely that the inconvenience was trifling; when, however, someone did come to visit the King of Montenegro, or some event of national importance such as the christening or marriage of a child had to be celebrated, the German legation, which was in every way more commodious, used to be borrowed for the party.

Another building of prominence was, or rather had been, the hotel, for this had caught fire some time before our visit and been totally demolished. Fortunately no one was staying there at the time; but, indeed, it would have been a peculiarly unfortunate coincidence if there had been, since fires and visitors are equally unusual events at Cetinje. Our arrival, therefore, in six dusty motor cars, had been carefully prepared for, and Montenegrins from all over the province had put on their best clothes and come into town to see the tourists and, if they could, make a little money. On the occasion of the first conducted tour arriving in Cetinje, some thirty or so years ago, the king himself had ridden out to greet them at the head of his household cavalry, and had so frightened the tourists by his salvoes of blank cartridges, a little wildly fired from the hip, that it was all the guides could do to persuade them to drive on into the town and attend the banquet prepared for them. There was no such demonstration for us, but the urchins of the country gave us a gentler welcome by throwing bunches of wild flowers into our laps as we drove past their houses.

As I have remarked, the hotel had lately been destroyed; luncheon was therefore served on trestle tables in the House of Parliament. It is only fair to say that this was no very serious degradation to the building, since even in the days of the kingdom it had combined a double office, being the legislature by day and the theatre by night. There was a stage at the end, surmounted by a crowned cypher, and on one of the walls hung a large, symbolic oil-painting, representing a man in Montenegrin national costume who held in one hand the fasces and in the other the mane of a live lion. This emblem of nationality reminded me strongly of the cartoons which appeared during the war. At one time, I remember, there was a strongly supported movement to make much of Montenegro. There was, if I remember rightly, a Montenegrin flag day, and 'Brave little Montenegro' for a very short time was a phrase of almost equal potency to 'Brave little Belgium' or 'Russian Steamroller'.

Luncheon was very bad indeed, even though it was cooked in the office of the commissar of police; the wine was a dark-coloured local vintage, not red but not exactly black, the colour one's fountain-pen makes when one dips it accidentally into the red inkpot; it was very sour and left a temporarily indelible stain on the tongue and teeth. After luncheon we walked round the broad lanes of the town, and visited the shops, where the stock of peasant textiles (indistinguishable from the products of Hampstead arts and crafts) was supplemented for the occasion by all kinds of curios, some of them crosses and bits of jewellery but mostly daggers and pistols with elaborately decorated hilts and butts. I presume that these were brought in by the owners and sold for them on heaven knows what exorbitant commission. It seemed to me rather pathetic to see them there, because among Balkan peoples these are often the only possessions of value, and are a real source of pride, being handed down from father to son, as symbols of family importance as well as of personal valour and independence. Most of them, I think, would have been of doubtful efficiency in prosecuting the blood feuds which enliven Montenegrin life. Indeed, I expect that it is futile to sentimentalize about them. Most likely the owners were saving up to buy cartridges for a stolen army rifle, and so snipe the neighbours in a more deadly manner from behind their pig-styes.

The drive back was quicker and far more hazardous than the ascent. There was just time for a swim in the fiord before the *Stella* sailed again.

SEVEN

During the next few days on our way back to Monte Carlo we were rarely out of sight of land for long. We stopped once more at Catania, Messina, and Naples. As before, a large party went up by train to Taormina. I remained on the *Stella* as I had done two months before. I cannot account for this disinclination to see Taormina. I think it was chiefly meanness and the fear of embarrassing some friends of mine whom I believed to be spending their honeymoon there. Also, the Straits of Messina are very beautiful, and it always seems odd to me that anyone, for any reason, should choose to travel by land when he can go by water.

I do not think I shall ever forget the sight of Etna at sunset; the mountain almost invisible in a blur of pastel grey, glowing on the top and then repeating its shape, as though reflected, in a wisp of grey smoke, with the whole horizon behind radiant with pink light, fading gently into a grey pastel sky. Nothing I have ever seen in Art or Nature was quite so revolting.

We passed Stromboli late in the evening. Everyone came out on deck in the hope of seeing an eruption, but was unrewarded.

We reached Naples on Ascension Day. This was always a great festival at my school. It was the only whole holiday in the year. We used to go in large bodies to a village called Bramber where there is a museum of stuffed monstrosities – two-headed hens, five-legged sheep, and so forth. It usually rained. It was also a great festival at Naples. The churches were all draped in white silk and blazing with electric-light bulbs. I was able to see much that had been locked away from me on my first visit.

I went to Pompeii, which everyone knows all about. I thought that the most interesting thing I saw was the plaster cast of the suffocated dog. I had heard a great deal about the pornographic frescoes which characterize many of the houses, and was surprised to find them, in most cases, mere scribbles, no better than D. H. Lawrence's, clearly not the work of the professional decorators who had made such an elegant job of the other rooms. Only one, in the house of Vetii, was at all amusing, and that only by the standard of American 'strip' draughtsmanship. In the most recently excavated streets, the discoveries have been left in their places, instead of being removed to the museum at Naples; this is naturally by far the most interesting quarter of the town. The guide who conducted us had a great clean-shaven jowl and pop-eyes; he might have been assassinated anywhere in mistake for Mussolini. It is very curious how the lower orders often grow to resemble the public figures of their generation. Gladstones are only just beginning to die out in England; there was a don at my college exactly like a prominent murderer.

The next day I drove out to luncheon at the Capucini Hotel at Amalfi, and home by Sorrento – a road of wonderful charm and variety.

On the night we left Naples there was a *diner d'adieu*. The most respected passenger made a speech proposing the health of the Captain and officers and thanking them for the safety and comfort of the voyage; the Captain responded and we all sang 'Auld Lang Syne'. Next morning we arrived at Monaco.

This was the end of the cruise. Luggage appeared on deck, supplemented by oddly shaped bundles of souvenirs piled up during the voyage. The passengers busied themselves in retrieving their passports, changing cheques, tipping the stewards, saying goodbye to the Captain and officers, saying goodbye to each other, and promising to meet again. My packing was only half done. I looked hopelessly at the heaps of clothes, books, and photographs on my bed. I thought despondently of the odious P.L.M. journey before me, of eating my meals in the restaurant car with my wine and my soup being rocked and splashed on the tablecloth, and the knives and forks jingling, and the servants jostling past in the corridors; of the sleepless night in a grossly expensive sleeper or propped upright in the corner of a carriage; of the foetid early morning air of the train, the unshaven grimy feeling; of creeping round Paris in the Ceinture; of the bleak quay at Calais and the bleaker quay at Dover, of all the dirt and indignity of travelling by rail. Then I pushed my trunk back under my bed.

The *Stella* had finished her Mediterranean season and was due to start back in two days to Norway to revictual for her summer cruises in the fiords. Her route now lay round the Spanish coast, touching at Algiers and Mallorca, to Harwich, a cruise of fourteen days. I decided to remain on board.

In the interval between the two cruises the ship was devoted to another terrific spring cleaning. I slept in my cabin and took my meals on shore. Monte Carlo was practically deserted; the Sporting Club was closed; the Russian ballet had packed up and left for their last season in London; the dress shops had either already closed or were advertising their end of the season sales; there were shutters up in most of the villas and hotels; a few invalids encumbered the promenades in their bath-chairs; Mr Rex Evans had ceased to sing. And I wondered, as I pottered about those serene and sunny streets or sat drowsily in the shade of the Casino Gardens, at that provision of destiny which has made rich people so rigidly liturgical in their movements that they will come to Monte Carlo in the snow because that is the time ordained for their arrival in rubric and calendar, and will leave as soon as it becomes habitable for their grubby great shambling cities in the north; and how unlike rich people are to the lilies of the field, who do not divide time by any metrical system, but will joyfully put out buds at the first intimation of spring, and lose them, almost immediately, in the intervening frost.

Two days later the new passengers came on board; there were three or four of us left from the preceding cruise, and we watched the new arrivals critically and decided that we did not think very much of them. They certainly did not look prepossessing next day, after a night of heavy seas in the Gulf of Lyons, but bore slightly discontented.faces, as though attributing the bad weather to negligence on the part of someone in authority. We sailed along the coast all the morning – while a charming Catalan whose acquaintance I had made, pointed out, very eagerly, the summer villas of his friends and relations–and reached Barcelona at two o'clock in the afternoon. At the mouth of the harbour and all along the breakwater lay a fleet of rafts, from which depended strings of mussels, fattening in sewage. We berthed alongside the quay in the inner basin.

It was a week too early for the Barcelona Exhibition, but there was plenty to see. There is a street called the Ramblas, with old houses and churches on each side and a broad promenade in the middle dividing the two narrow lanes of traffic. This promenade is full of seats and trees and kiosks for selling newspapers and cigarettes and picture-postcards; at all hours of the day it is full of soldiers and townspeople, saluting and gossiping, but its chief beauty is the flower stalls, which colour and perfume the whole length of the street. These are best about midday, before the stock has been depleted by purchasers, or grown dusty and limp. There is a cathedral of Spanish Gothic, the windows of which have been reduced to little slits and peep-holes of stained glass; the darkness of the interior is almost impenetrable, and the little light there is, is so unnatural that it seemed not to be a real building at all but a stage setting – perhaps for the temptation of Marguerite in *Faust*, or for *The Hunchback of Notre Dame*, or the final act of some historical drama in which the heroine, penitent, renounces the world and becomes a nun – the sentimentalized caricature of the Gothic of Chartres or Beauvais. There is a frightful hill called Tibidabo, laid out as a pleasure garden with a restaurant and café, a hall of slot machines, an unfinished oratory of fantastic design, and a Great Wheel. There is an excellent taxi company called 'David', whose drivers speak French and refuse tips; there are also various freelance taxi drivers of menacing aspect, who speak no foreign language, manipulate the taxi-meter to their own advantage, and demand large tips. There are numerous fine houses in the old part of the town, with wrought-iron gates and pretty courtyards. There is, I believe, though I was too tired after our rough passage to investigate it, a riotous night life in the streets round the docks. I had two meals on shore at quiet restaurants and found the prices high and the cooking execrable. The wine, however, was quite good. At one of the restaurants, a very humble place, little more than a cabman's eating-house, I saw a young private soldier drink from a flask that had a spout, finely pointed at the end, protruding from its side. He held it at arm's length, tilting it so that a very delicate stream of wine shot from it with some force. This he caught in his mouth by negligently protruding his lower lip. The wine splashed against his teeth and gurgled down his throat without a drop being spilled. Then, with a deft twist of the wrist, he stopped the flow, catching the last drips, and passed the flask across the table to his companion, who drank in the same manner, but more clumsily, directing the stream first into his eye and then down his chin, to the delight of everyone in the restaurant. It looks very difficult to drink like that, and is, I believe, more difficult than it looks, but it must be very delicious when one has learned.

But the glory and delight of Barcelona, which no other town in the world can offer, is the architecture of Gaudi. In England we scarcely know the meaning of Art Nouveau. Mr John Betjeman, the chief living authority on the subject, traces it chiefly in the decorative motive of the roots of the water-lily, which became prominent in this country at about the time of William Morris's death; I have seen pewter work, too, of about 1900, in which tulips and dock leaves have been very happily rendered; there are stencil designs in some early numbers of the *Studio* in which one can discern the repressed but resilient aspirations of the movement, but with us, as with the Parisians, decadence proved the more vital force. The peacock's feather and the green carnation outshine the tulip and the water-lily root. Then, after a warm but inconclusive flirtation with Holland – when painters made heavily patterned pictures of windmills and umber sails, and put tiles round their hearths and pot-bellied jugs of burnished copper in their windows – English decorative fancy went whirling off among timber and thatch and black old oak. But this was not the case with the Catalans who responded to the movement with all the zeal of their exuberant but wholly undiscriminating nature. They never concerned themselves with the Decadence or with archaism. Art Nouveau came to them at a time of commercial expansion and political unrest, and they took it to themselves and made it their own, even christening it and importing it into Florida under their own name, as the Neo-Catalan style. In its new guise it has even, in recent years, come back to England. Near to where I am writing this, on the south coast of England, there is a small colony of villas and bungalows extending from Bognor Regis for about a mile along the edge of the beach. They are mostly empty during the winter months, so that I can lean on their gates and study them without causing annoyance or suspicion, and in their very new and, I trust, impermanent structure I have been able to discern many features that are fundamentally Neo-Catalan. There is the same eagerness to attract attention, though this, I think, may be more a commercial than an artistic impulse. They are built not as homes, but as holiday pavilions to be let on short leases at extravagant rents during the bathing season; their aim is to catch the eye with a prominent exterior and leave the interior to chance, in the confidence that the tenants will spend most of the day sprawling on the sand. They exhibit the same irresponsible confusion of architectural styles, here Gothic, here Tudor, here Classical. They exhibit the same abhorrence of an unvariegated line, whenever it is structurally possible substituting machicolation or sweeping curvature. They exhibit the same predilection for very bright colours and iridescent surfaces, more particularly those achieved by glazed tiles or a mosaic of broken china and pebbles embedded in cement. This last is one of the chief decorative devices of Neo-Catalan architecture; there are examples of it sparkling and blazing all over Barcelona, but Gaudi alone was able to use it with precision and enterprise and make of it the craft which, in New York, is reverently known as 'Tiffany bathroom'.

Gaudi bears to these anonymous contractors and job-builders something of the same relation as do the masters of Italian baroque to the rococo decorators of the Pompadour's boudoir, or Ronald Firbank to the author of *Frolic Wind*. What in them is frivolous, superficial, and *chic* is in him structural and essential; in his work is apotheosized all the writhing, bubbling, convoluting, convulsing soul of the Art Nouveau.

I could discover very little about his life save that it began in Barcelona, was for the most part spent there, and ended there less than five years ago, when the aged and partially infirm master was run down and killed by an electric tram-car in the main boulevard of the town. In his later years he did very little creative work, devoting his failing energies to supervising the construction of the great Church of the Holy Family, which I shall shortly describe. The period of his grossest and wildest output is the last two decades of the last century; it was then that his art, cautiously maturing, broke through all preconceived bounds of order and propriety, and coursed wantonly over the town, spattering its riches on all sides like mud.

But, indeed, in one's first brush with Gaudi's genius, it is not so much propriety that is outraged as one's sense of probability. My interest in him began on the morning of my second and, unfortunately, my last day in Barcelona. I was walking alone and without any clear intention in my mind, down one of the boulevards when I saw what, at first, I took to be part of the advertising campaign of the Exhibition. On closer inspection I realized that it was a permanent building, which to my surprise turned out to be the offices of the Turkish Consulate. Trees were planted in front of it along the pavement, hiding the lower storeys. It was the roof which chiefly attracted my attention, since it was coloured peacock-blue and built in undulations, like a rough sea petrified; the chimneys, too, were of highly coloured glazed earthenware, and they were twisted and bent in all directions like very gnarled fruit-trees. The front of the building, down to the level of the second row of windows, was made of the mosaic of broken china I have described above, but thoughtfully planned so that the colours merged in delicate gradations from violet and blue to peacock-green and gold. The eaves overhung in irregular, amorphous waves, in places attenuated into stalactites of coloured porcelain; the effect was that of a clumsily iced cake. I cannot describe it more accurately than that because, dazzled and blinded by what I subsequently saw, my impression of this first experience, though deep, is somewhat indistinct. I went all round it with a camera trying to find an aspect I could photograph, but the trees and the sun combined to frustrate me.

I knew now what I wanted to see in Barcelona; hiring one of the David taxis, I made the driver understand that I wanted to go to any other building like this one. He took me to a large apartment house not far away, called, I think, the Casa Milá y Camps. I verified the fact later at a photograph shop that this was by the same architect as the Turkish Consulate, and that his name was Gaudi. I was able to take snapshots of this building which I have before me as I write, but the impression they give is far less eccentric than the reality. It has the same undulating roof of coloured tiles, but Gaudi has here introduced the innovation that the curves of the sky-line do not correspond in any way at all to the curves of the top of the walls. The chimney-stacks are all different in design, some being decorated in spirals, others in diamonds, others in vertical ribs, but of somewhat the same shape, like great bee-hives, from the top of which protrude little asymmetrical chimney-pots. The walls of the building, which stands at a corner, are faced with rough sandstone, pierced by six courses of windows. These are made to look like caves, having no sharply defined outlines or any straight line anywhere about them, sides, top, and bottom being all wildly and irrelevantly curved, as if drawn by a faltering hand. The ground plan, too, is designed with the same undulating boundaries. Perhaps the most unexpected thing about this building is the ironwork; the front door is composed of glass panes set in an iron frame of uncompromising irregularity, like the cuts in a jigsaw puzzle or the divisions in that thing known to gardeners as a 'crazy pavement', while outside many of the windows have wrought-iron balustrades that are fearless tangles of twisted metal, like the wreckage of an aeroplane that has fallen burning from a great height and has suddenly been cooled with hosings of cold water.

There are undoubtedly other houses by Gaudi in Barcelona, and somewhere in the district, I was told, one could see a bishop's palace of his design, but in the short time at my disposal I was obliged to concentrate myself upon his two major works, the Parc Güell and the Templo de la Sagrada Familia. Both of these lie some little way out of the town. Parc Güell is a public garden and recreation ground; it is also the name of the surrounding suburb, so that it was a little time before I could make my taxi-driver understand which I wanted; this difficulty was increased by my own ignorance. I had simply been told that there was Gaudi work at the Parc Güell; no more. We drove up several streets of villas, all extravagantly Neo-Catalan but lacking in just that quality which I had already learned to recognize as the master's. The moment we came into sight of the entrance gates of the gardens there was no more doubt; this was the real thing. I paid off the taxi and entered up a double flight of china-mosaic steps, between curving machicolated walls, decorated in a gay check pattern of coloured tiles, at the base of which was a little fountain and a kind of totem pole of mosaic.

I think that the whole gardens were laid out by Gaudi; certainly all the architectural features are unmistakably his. There is a great terrace on which the children play games, with a fine crinkled edge of the typical broken china mosaic; there is a battlemented wall built of rough stones and clinkers, and embellished with plaques of the word 'Güell' in contorted, interlacing letters; there is a kind of pergola supported on a colonnade of clinker pillars set askew and at all angles to each other; there is a turret, surmounted by a wrought-iron stand supporting a cross; there is a little lodge that is a gem of Gaudism, looking like a fairy cabin from the worst kind of Rackhamesque picture book.

Only a small part has as yet been built of the great Church of the Holy Family, which was to have been Gaudi's supreme achievement, and unless some eccentric millionaire is moved to interpose in the near future, in spite of the great sums that have already been squandered upon it, the project will have to be abandoned. The vast undertaking was begun with very small funds and relied entirely upon voluntary contributions for its progress. The fact that it has got as advanced as it has, is a testimony to the great enthusiasm it has aroused among the people of the country, but enthusiasm and contributions have dwindled during the last twenty years, until only ten men are regularly employed, most of their time being taken up in repairing the damage caused to the fabric by its exposure; there are already menacing cracks in the towers; immense sums would be required to finish the building on the scale in which it was planned, and the portions already constructed fatally compromise any attempt at modification. It seems to me certain that it will always remain a ruin – and a highly dangerous one unless the towers are removed before they fall down.

All that is finished at present is the crypt, a part of the cloisters, the south door, two of the towers, and part of the east wall. There is a model in the crypt of the finished building, which was shown in Paris at one of the International Exhibitions but did not attract any great international support. The church is to be circular with a straight, gabled south front, forming a tangent touching the circumference, not, as might be supposed, at its centre, but at a point some way to the east of the central main door; beyond the high altar is to be a baptistry with a very high, pointed dome, fretted and presumably glazed.

There is a sacristan employed to show visitors over the building, and it is only by their contributions that the work continues at all. He told me that it makes a very strong appeal to the peasants of the neighbourhood, who come in large numbers to wonder at the cleverness of the carving. Tourists for the most part are unsympathetic, he said, expressing their impatience with the eccentricities of 'modern art'. I do not say that if I were rich I could not find a better way of devoting my fortune, but I do think that it would be a pity to allow this astonishing curiosity to decay. I feel it would be a graceful action on the part of someone who was a little wrong in the head to pay for its completion.

I could easily have employed a happy fortnight at Barcelona tracking down further examples of Gaudism. He designed many things besides houses, I believe, making it his special province to conceive designs for tables and chairs and other objects of common utility which would render them unfit for their ostensible purposes. He is a great example, it seems to me, of what art-for-art's-sake can become when it is wholly untempered by considerations of tradition or good taste. Picabia in Paris is another example; but I think it would be more exciting to collect Gaudis.

There is a large book on Gaudi published in Barcelona which I could not at the time afford to buy; nor, if I had bought it, should I have been able to read it, since it is written in Spanish. But I should dearly like to have gone round with this book, identifying the illustrations and making photographs and sketches of my own; perhaps even to have read a paper or produced a monograph upon the subject.

But the *Stella* was due to sail that evening, and my passage was booked to England.

EIGHT

We had rather a nasty crossing to Mallorca, where we spent the next day. I have heard people being very eloquent about the charm of this island, but I must confess that I found it disappointing. It may be that, after moving as rapidly from place to place as we had been doing lately, one's palate becomes vitiated with an excess of variety, so that one misses the subtler and more fugitive qualities which reveal themselves shyly to more leisured travellers, and one requires the pungent flavour of Gaudi to arouse one's appetite for further sight-seeing. Or it may be that those who have come to love the Balearic Isles so deeply are inexperienced, and judge them by contrast with the Isles of Wight or of Man, or perhaps they have been fortunate there in love and see them suffused by their own memories. Whatever the reason, I was a little bored. Mallorca seemed a pretty, sleepy little island and Palma a pretty, sleepy little town; for the same kind of attraction I rather prefer Tarascon or Wells. I walked about the town in the morning and saw the cathedral, where there was nothing to see, and the market where there was nothing to buy. I had an *apéritif* in a shady café in the main square; it was rather expensive; nothing in Palma was as cheap as I had been led to suppose; the taxis were almost as exorbitant as those of Oxford. In the afternoon I went for a drive into the interior of the island, along lanes bordered with thorn hedges and banks of rich red loam, like the west of England. The taxi-driver's brother was gardener at the country villa of one of the important citizens of the town; he took me to see the garden, which was built on the side of a little valley, with two or three springs bubbling up in it and falling down in ornamental cascades to the stream at the bottom of the hill; the woods on the opposing slope were full of nightingales. The villa itself was a lovely old house, built round a *patio* in the Spanish manner; behind it the hill ascended steeply, with rocky paths, rose-trees, grottoes, and more waterfalls and rivulets. One grotto had a marble Venus inside it, and all round the walls, and in the ceiling and floor, were little concealed jets, which could be turned on all together, suddenly, from outside, drenching Venus and the visitor in a dozen delicate spouts of water. I have seen bathrooms equipped like this in the houses of rich people in England. This form of practical joke was not uncommon in Europe in the eighteenth century, but I believe that it was originally learned from the Moors. In the Alcazar Palace at Seville there is a maze set in one of the tessallated pavements, the centre and goal of which is a little fountain. As the unwary guest leaned over it to trace his way through the intricate corners and blind alleys of the puzzle, his host would turn on the tap and souse him. It is now out of order, and perhaps is deliberately left in this condition so that the custodian shall not be tempted to bring ridicule on the tourists. I think that, if one had nothing else to do, it would be fun to collect practical jokes of this kind. I know a house in Ireland which has in its hall a carved oak chair of nineteenth-century construction; as one sits down in it, iron clamps fly out from the arms and imprison one's thighs inextricably until one is released by a trigger from behind; this toy can be very painful indeed to stout people; nowadays ingenuity seems to take milder forms, mostly in association with music boxes which play inside decanters or cigarette boxes or rolls of toilet paper.

It was the Norwegian Independence Day, and the *Stella* was dressed with hundreds of little flags. That evening there were speeches at dinner, and after the dancing a very heavenly party, to which I was invited, given by the officers and the Scandinavian passengers. The first officer made a patriotic speech in Norwegian and then in English, and then he made a speech in English in praise of England and then translated his speech into Norwegian. Then I made a speech in English in praise of Norway, and one of the passengers translated my speech into Norwegian; then she made a speech in English and Norwegian in praise of England and Norway and quoted Kipling. It was all delightful. Then we went down to the lower deck, where the crew were having a tremendous supper of Norwegian *delicatessen* and sugar cakes and champagne; one of them was on a rostrum made of flags; he was delivering a patriotic speech. Then we all drank each other's health and danced; it was by no means a calm sea. Then we went up to the Captain's cabin and ate a dish called *eggdosis*, but I do not know how it was spelt. It was made of eggs and sugar and brandy whipped up into a firm cream. Then we went to the cabin of the lady who had translated my speech – she had one of the suites-de-luxe, of the kind which Geoffrey and Juliet had occupied – and there we made more speeches, oddly enough most of them in French.

I woke up feeling a little ill after Independence Day, and found that we had arrived in Algiers and were berthed alongside the Quai de Marine in the Port de Commerce, and that the deck was already covered with stalls as though for a charity bazaar. They were selling filigree gold jewellery, binoculars, and carpets. The jewellery was vile; the binoculars were mostly of well-known makes and, being duty free, were astonishingly cheap; several passengers bought pairs, but I do not know whether or not they succeeded in getting them past the Customs at Harwich. The carpets, too, were very cheap; some were shiny, of European manufacture; others were native workmanship of rough striped wool like horse blankets. The water in the harbour was dense with floating refuse; young men swam about, butting and churning back with their arms the scum of empty bottles, sodden paper, grape-fruit skins, and kitchen waste, and calling for coins to be thrown to them.

The town is built along the slopes of the west side of the Bay of Algiers. Except for the little triangle of mean streets around and below the Kasbar quarter, it has grown up in the second half of the last century on a typically French provincial model. There is a Place de la République, planted with magnolia-trees and bamboos, surrounded by cafés and restaurants; broad, arcaded boulevards lead out of this, with offices, shops, and apartment houses. French posters are on all the hoardings, advertising Peugeot, Dubonnet, Savon Palmolive, Citroën, Galeries Lafayette; an expanse of garden suburb stretches out to the south; there is a fine park laid out with tropical plants; a Bois de Boulogne; a Shakespeare Chemin; a nine-hole golf course and a Chemin du Golfe; the wooded hills above the town are dotted with larger villas, barracks, and forts.

A fortnight before our arrival the Foreign Legion had been in quarters here, but had now been moved upcountry. I should have liked to see this company of exiled chivalry – all, I like to think, suffering for the good name of others, all of exalted and romantic origin. The taxi-driver to whom I spoke of them gave an unenthusiastic account. They got so little pay, he said, that there was nothing they could ever afford to do, except to stand about at the street corners and spit; they were for the most part tough, undersized young criminals of very limited intellect; he was glad to see the backs of them. But taxi-drivers, as a race, are always constitutionally misanthropic.

An expedition drove off from the *Stella* to visit a valley of monkeys, but I remained behind in the town, where there seemed quite enough to employ one's attention for a couple of days. It was particularly interesting after Port Said, which, except for the determining fact of French administration, should have had much in common. The great difference was the apparent absence of racial and colour distinctions in Algiers. It is by no means a predominantly Moorish population. Baedeker gives the figures in 1911 as 33,200 Mohammedans, 12,500 Jews, and 35,200 Europeans, mostly Italians and Spaniards. In the last twenty years the balance has been shifted still further against the Mohammedans by the steady influx of French traders and officials and the development of the higher slopes as a winter resort for the rich of all nations. Even the Kasbar, the ancient Oriental quarter, is invaded by Maltese and low-class Mediterraneans of various races. The Moors, however, have made no attempt at imitation, either of the clothes or manners of the Europeans. There is no Kemalist nonsense about votes for women and bowler hats. The men remain polygamous, and walk about the streets gravely conversing with each other, very dignified figures indeed, in large, padded turbans and long cloaks, carrying tall walking-sticks; while their wives trot behind, veiled in white, their eyes circled with smears of paint and their fingers steeped in henna. The men mix absolutely freely with Europeans of their own class; the white porters and street scavengers exchange cigarette ends with their coloured colleagues, while, in the chief cafés, handsomely robed Moorish landowners sit unembarrassed at the next tables to naval and military officers and frock-coated *légionnaires*, listening to the band, drinking their vermouth and Cassis, reading the French journals, and exchanging greetings on all sides. What is it, I wonder, which gives the Anglo-Saxons, alone among the colonists of the world, this ungenerous feeling of superiority over their neighbours? Why did the British residents at Port Said warn me against the hotels which might harbour 'gyppies'? At the restaurant where I lunched on the second morning, there was a delightful party at the next table – a dapper little Frenchman and his wife and three Moors with long beards, great aquiline noses, and very humorous, wrinkled eyes. One of these was host. They were all clearly enjoying their luncheon immensely, and drinking a lot of local *vin rosé*. The Frenchwoman was flirting mildly with her host, and her husband was making very successful jokes which I could not quite overhear, although I strained all my attention to do so.

This was a very charming restaurant. I omitted to record the name in my notebook, but it is easy enough to find, a little way down the Boulevard de la République. There are tables inside and on the pavement, among shrubs in pots, overlooking the harbour. It was very Marseillais in character; an elderly woman stood behind a table opening crumpled little bright green oysters; there were heaps of rather dangerous-looking lobsters and *écrevisses*. I ate *bouillabaisse* and *oeufs la Turque*, and drank some Algerian white wine. I do not believe that Algerian wine is really very nice. It was evidently a very popular restaurant; every table was occupied; but perhaps that was because it happened to be Whit Sunday.

After luncheon I climbed rather heavily up to the Kasbar. There is a fine view from there over the town and harbour and the whole Bay of Algiers; the houses are very old and the alleys narrow and precipitous; it has that vivid street life that one sees in every old town which has a slum quarter inaccessible to traffic; there was one street and a little terrace given up to houses of ill-fame – all very gay with bright paint and tiles, and crowded thick at every door and window with plain, obese young women in gaudy clothes. If I had come there fresh from England I should have found it amusing enough, but as a spectacle of Oriental life it was less exciting than Cairo on Bajiram night, and as an example of medieval town-planning less formidable than the Manderaggio at Valletta.

There was very little begging or street hawking except the inevitable swarm of boot-cleaners, and no native dragomans. Except on the harbour front one could walk about unmolested; there, however, one had to run the gauntlet of a great number of guides – nasty, jaunty young men for the most part, dressed in European suits and straw hats, bow ties, and Charlie Chaplin moustaches; they spoke French and some English, and were, I imagine, of vaguely European extraction. Their particular trade was organizing parties to see native dances – *fêtes Mauresques* – and an intolerable nuisance they were over it. Many of the passengers from the *Stella* went off with them and came back with very different reports of the entertainment. Some appeared to have seen decorous and perfectly genuine performances in the courtyards of one or other of the medieval Moorish houses; they described a native band with drums and wind instruments and a troupe of veiled dancing girls who went through the figures of various traditional tribal dances; they said it was a little monotonous, but they seemed quite satisfied with their evening. Another party, including two Englishwomen, were led to the top floor of a house of ill-fame, where they were sat round the walls of a tiny room. Here they waited for some time in the light of a small oil lamp, becoming more and more uneasy, until the curtains of the door were suddenly thrust aside and a very large, elderly Jewess pranced in among them, quite naked except for a little cheap jewellery, and proceeded to perform a *danse de ventre* on the few yards of the floor that separated them. The verdict of one of the Englishwomen on this experience was: 'Well, I am quite glad in a way to have seen it, but I should certainly never wish to go again.' Her companion refused to discuss the subject at all, from any angle, with anyone, and for the rest of the voyage entirely avoided the company of the gentlemen who had escorted her that evening.

But there was one party who had a still sadder time of it. They were five Scots people in early middle age, three women and two men, inter-related in some way that I never had occasion to define. These were caught by a very shady guide who took them up to the Kasbar in a taxi-cab. He charged them 200 francs for this drive, which they politely paid without question. He then took them to a house in a blind alley, knocked on the door three times, and excited their uneasiness by saying, 'This is very dangerous. You are safe as long as you are with me, but on no account get separated or I cannot answer for the consequences.' They were admitted one at a time and charged a 100 francs each. The door was shut behind them and they were led down to a cellar. The guide explained to them that they must order coffee, which they did at the cost of 20 francs a head. Before they had tasted it a revolver shot sounded just outside the door.

'Run for your lives,' said the guide.

They scampered out and found their taxi, which, by apparent good fortune, was waiting for them.

'No doubt the ladies are feeling unsettled by their experience. Would they like a little cognac?'

He then directed the car, which cost another 200 francs, to one of the ordinary cafés of the town and gave them each a tot of *eau-de-vie*. He settled the bill for them and explained that it had come to 25 francs a head and 10 francs for the tip.

'That is the advantage of coming with me,' he explained. 'I do the tips for you and you are not put upon. There are many cheats in this town who would take advantage of your inexperience if you were alone.'

He then saw them back to the ship, reminding them discreetly that the fees for his evening's services were 100 francs or whatever they liked to make it. They were still so bewildered and agitated that they gave him a hundred and fifty, thanking him very much and congratulating themselves on the narrow escape they had had. Only later, talking it over among themselves, did the suspicion arise that perhaps the charges had been unduly heavy, and that the house from which they had made their escape might, in fact, be the guide's own home, and that his wife or small son or a kindly neighbour had fired the pistol for them.

I think it did them great credit that they did not conceal this dismal story, but told it to everyone on board, half resentfully but half humorously.

'I'd like to go back and have a few words with that merchant,' remarked the men of the party, but, alas, by that time we had left Algiers.

We sailed that night and were at sea until late the next evening, when we came in to Malaga. It was cold and grey and windy all that day. It is depressing to wake up to rough weather with the plates creaking and doors banging and things rolling about overhead. Many people stayed in their cabins. Those that came up sat about moodily, wrapped in rugs, with novels which they left open across their knees for long periods at a time. A few of the sturdier ones attempted deck games, but the movement of the ship took all pleasure from them as competitions, leaving only the satisfaction of bravado. I am a fairly good sailor and did not actually feel ill. I must admit, however, that I had very little appetite that day for food, wine, or tobacco. At the best, rough weather is profoundly irritating to the nerves, as it renders almost all activity laborious and ineffectual. I was very glad to see harbour lights and people walking about under the trees, watching us as we came in.

We spent two days here, to enable those who wished to go up to Granada. I stayed on board, mainly because I was short of money; there is very little to see or do in Malaga, though it is an agreeable, compact little town, smelling strongly of burnt olive oil and excrement. It looks very pretty from the sea, with an avenue of trees along the front, and behind them the white limestone cathedral and steep little hills, one of them crowned by some dissolute fortifications. But one has seen the best of it before one lands. The cathedral is a nice clean piece of sixteenth-century architecture, still unfinished, though work went on at it intermittently until the middle of the eighteenth century. It reminded me strongly of the chapel at Hertford College, evoking long suppressed memories to me of all those gentle and wise men who directed my youth with who can tell what insight and sympathy, and of all the smug, sheep-faced undergraduates praying for success in their pass schools, and above them, crouching in his stall, the venerable figure of my history tutor, ill at ease in his starched white surplice, biting his nails, and brooding, I have no doubt, on all the good he intended for each one of us. But these were the most flimsy of ghosts; there was no one like that in the cathedral at Malaga; only a riotous troop of begging choir boys, and paralysed old women, and a dull verger.

Two streets to the east of the cathedral is a little hill called Alcazabar, covered with tumbledown cottages and some indistinguishable Moorish remains. This is peopled with gypsies and goats, and it is from here, when the wind is in that quarter, that the town gets its smell.

There is a wine called Malaga, a species of dark, sweet sherry, which I have drunk and disliked in England. I drank some here, hoping it would be better, but found it very nasty. It is drunk locally in big bumpers as an *apéritif*, in accordance with that paradoxical Latin taste which prescribes something sweet and thick and pungent at this time of the evening; though whether it is preferable to cloy the palate in this way, or to paralyse it with iced spirits in the fashion of my own country, I leave for the gourmets to decide. There were two or three clubs in the town, along the main thoroughfare, but these were built like cafés, open to the street, with only a low rail between the passers-by and the members; stout, easy-looking men who sat all day in armchairs, smoking cheroots and staring at the traffic. No doubt this is a regular institution in Andalusia; it was new to me and seemed noteworthy and laudable.

In spite of the bad weather we had encountered on the way there, our two days at Malaga turned out bright and warm. There was an excellent bathing-place a mile or so down the coast, to which I went with the second officer and a few of the passengers; there were bright little cabins and a steep beach and a café-restaurant, but the water was still deadly cold. On my second afternoon I drove out in a one-horse carriage to a pretty park and garden of the Hacienda de San José and the villa of La Concepcion, and walked about on grey shingle paths under semi-tropical trees between brilliant green banks, scattered in places with Roman antiquities of broken marble.

Late the second evening the expedition returned from Granada, dusty and tired and rather cross. As soon as they were safely embarked we sailed again, this time through calm waters, and arrived during the early hours of the morning at Gibraltar.

All over the world there are rock formations in which people profess to see the likeness of natural objects – heads of crusaders, dogs, cattle, petrified beldams, etc. There is an idea, started, I believe, by Thackeray, that the Rock of Gibraltar looks like a lion. 'It is the very image,' he said, 'of an enormous lion, crouched between the Atlantic and the Mediterranean, and set there to guard the passage for its British mistress.' Everyone else on board was instantly struck by the felicity of this image, so I suppose that it must be due to some deficiency in my powers of observation that to me it appeared like a great slab of cheese and like nothing else.

An English policeman with helmet, whistle, truncheon, and rolled mackintosh cape was on duty at the landing-stage. I think this man pleased the English passengers more than anything they had seen in their travels. 'It makes one feel so safe inside,' said one of the ladies; but I cannot for the life of me think what she meant by that.

I will not say that I did not know any town could be so ugly as the town of Gibraltar; to say that would be to deny many bitter visits in the past to Colwyn Bay, Manchester, and Stratford-on-Avon; but I will say that I had forgotten much, and that Gibraltar was a shock, and sudden sharp reminder of what I was returning to. In the past three months I had seen so many towns of widely different origin and circumstance, but all distinguished in some way by fine architecture or a gracious setting or a seemly and individual habit of life. Baedeker, always slow to condemn, remarks of Gibraltar that 'the streets are narrow and dark and are relieved by few squares ... the cleanness of the town and the absence of beggars produce a pleasant impression' and of the Anglican cathedral he reticently confines himself to the statement that it is 'built in the Moorish style'; he reminds those in search of entertainment that a military band plays near the Assembly Rooms on Sundays and Wednesdays between the hours of three and five in the afternoon. His bald, unemphasized account of the little peninsula is one of the most able passages in the whole of his works, and suggests more censure than all the adjectives I can assemble.

The only place that I can think of at all like the town of Gibraltar, is Shoreham-by-Sea in Sussex, but this comparison will mean little, I suppose, to most English people. For those, however, who have at any time had occasion to pass through it, or, worse, to stop there, I will add this modification – that they must think of Gibraltar as a Shoreham deprived of its two churches, and scoured of all the ramshackle, haphazard characteristics which make it relatively tolerable. It is Shoreham, with a touch of Aldershot, transplanted to the east coast of Scotland or the north coast of Wales; Shoreham emptied of those mild, nondescript old men with beards, who potter about the side of the estuary, spitting into the mud flats; Shoreham never brightened by those passing charabancs and car-loads of south coast trippers.

I walked for some time about those very clean streets, feeling that there could be no town in the world without something of interest somewhere. The shop windows displayed little except seedy shaving brushes and tarnished cutlery and indefinable objects stitched on to

cards; there were chemists' shops selling English aperients and patent
pills; a paper-shop selling threepenny novelettes and twopenny week-
lies; a few curiosity shops with a stock oddly composed of little
Victorian and Edwardian knick-knacks – descended presumably
from officers' villas – and flaring modern embroideries and beaten
metal from Tangier. There was a tobacconist selling Dunhill pipes
and tobacco-jars ornamented with regimental and naval devices. I
passed some sailors' wives standing near a milliner's window; they
shrank as I passed as though I had brought with me some of the
polluted air of Malaga. Most of them, I learned later, keep strictly
to their houses when there are 'trippers about', like Hampstead
residents on bank-holidays.

As I was walking along very disconsolately I found a notice which
said, 'To Brighter 'Bralter ☞ '. I followed it for some way until
I came to another, similar announcement, and so, in pursuit of
pleasure, I began a kind of lugubrious treasure hunt, following these
clues through the length of that town. At last I came to the South
Port Gate and a neat little cemetery, where are buried a number of
men who fell at Trafalgar. Many of the graves were of pretty,
Wedgwood pattern, with urns and delicate carved plaques. Somewhat farther ahead, in a kind of recreation ground, preparations were
being made with tents and awnings for some kind of gymkhana. I
felt, however, that the posters had at least led me to the one.tolerable
spot on the Rock. In the afternoon I went for a little drive in a horse-
carriage, to a dismal neck of sand, quarter of a mile broad, called
Neutral Ground, which divides the English and Spanish territory.
I wonder what would be the legal consequences of putting up some
bungalows there and starting a little lawless colony.

Gibraltar claims this other distinction, that it is the only place in
Europe inhabited by wild monkeys. I saw none, but they are said
to frequent the higher slopes in large numbers; indeed, at one time
they became a great cause of offence, pinching and biting the
garrison, snatching at hats, firing off cannon at unsuitable moments,
chattering impudently in the faces of high officials, and openly
demonstrating the facts of life before the officers' children; the
governor accordingly had them exterminated, upon which such an
outcry went up on all sides, demanding where were the traditions
of English seamanship, and what would become of our domination

in the Atlantic, and how could Gib. be looked on as the key to the Mediterranean, now that it was robbed of its monkeys, that he was obliged to import a fresh stock from Africa, who rapidly repopulated the Rock and restored popular confidence.

Nothing could have been less like Gibraltar than our next stop, Seville. We arrived at the mouth of the Guadalquivir at about noon, but had to wait for some time, as ships of the *Stella*'s capacity are only able to cross the bar at high-water. The river is navigable as far as Seville by vessels of twenty-three foot draught. I should think that we came very near to the maximum. The only other ship we met of the same size was the *Meteor*, a cruising steam-ship belonging to the same company as ourselves; she was berthed next to us by the river bank, and some of us went over to visit her; many of the *Stella*'s officers had been transferred from her, and I had heard a great deal about her from them, who often spoke of their experiences on 'the good old *Meteor*', and also from my elder brother, who had once travelled in her to Norway; she is a pretty ship, built on much the same lines as the *Stella*, though less up to date in her equipment.

It is over fifty miles to Seville from the open sea, and we had necessarily to make slow progress in the narrow, meandering river. The banks on either side were low; at first we travelled between sandy flats covered with rough pasture and herds of black cattle; later these gave place to trees and occasional farms and villages, the inhabitants of which turned out to wave; the water was brown and quite opaque, like breakfast coffee, as I have sometimes found the bathwater in remote country houses. After the blustering of the Atlantic this gentle progression was at first soothing, then irritating, and then towards evening very soothing again. It was quite dark by the time we reached our destination and moored against the grassy right bank of the river; this, too, seemed odd after so many diverse harbours, to be lying alongside a towing path, like a college barge on the Isis.

As I remarked when I first set out in the *Stella*, one of the chief advantages of this sort of travelling is that it enables one to sample a great many places quite effortlessly, and choose those one wants to return to afterwards. Seville is certainly a town for a prolonged visit. In the two days that we were there, I was only able to get a glimpse at a few of the obvious show places and a few hints at the life of the people. This year, or next year, or later, I shall go back there. At present it seems to me impertinent to write very much about it. It is certainly one of the most lovely cities I have ever seen; only a general diffidence about the superlative prevents me from saying the most lovely. I can think of many with more lovely things in them, but none that has the same sweetness and refinement combined with activity and good sense; it seems to avoid every sort of vulgarity, even that of the professional beauty. I did not begin to master the geography of the town, and remember it now in a series of isolated magic lantern slides. The cathedral is magnificent; one of the finest in Europe; a great, spacious, Gothic church full of superb sculpture hidden in dark corners and behind metal gates. The dome was never a great success technically, as it has twice fallen in since it was originally built; the last restoration was by Casanova, in the late eighties, and it is hoped that he has succeeded in making it relatively permanent; just outside the cathedral is a large *patio*, once the courtyard of a mosque, in which hangs a stuffed crocodile sent by the Sultan of Egypt to Alfonso the Learned, with a suit for the hand of his daughter.

The Alcazar palace is very pretty, with delicately carved wood, open plaster work like lace, and beautiful Oriental tiles; it must be a great joy to those who can feel any genuine enthusiasm for Moorish work, and it is worth noticing that this, like most of the best Moorish houses in Seville, was constructed after the Christian occupation. The gardens of the Alcazar, with pavilion, grotto, and fountains, cannot help delighting the most hard-boiled Westerner.

The other most famous building is the Giralda, a square tower built of Roman brick; this was originally the minaret of the mosque, but the Christians added a belfry, a small dome, and a bronze figure of Faith. At the time of our visit, it was illuminated in the evenings by floodlights, in honour of the Spanish-American Exposition.

This exhibition had only just opened, and many of the buildings were still unfinished. It must not be supposed, however, that the project had been hurriedly or frivolously undertaken. The 1913 edition of Baedeker's *Spain and Portugal* mentions that large portions of the park were at that time closed for the preparations. The war delayed matters, but after the war work was begun again, deliberately and thoroughly. Everything was done on a solid and permanent basis. The pavilions are not mere lath and plaster erections, designed to last a dry summer; they are massive palaces of brick and stone, which are to be used later, I believe, for an Andalusian University. We were presented on landing with a prettily decorated prospectus written in English, which remarked: 'Five hundred years from now the descendants of those who visit this Exposition will see with their own eyes these very same buildings, mellowed by the passing ages, but equal to their present grandeur in lines and in massive construction.' Some of the buildings certainly will profit by mellowing, being at present very gay indeed in bright patterned brick work and coloured tiles; a little too gay, perhaps, for their 'massive construction' and the academic future ordained for them. Their contents, however, were magnificent. The Colonial and South American pavilions were not yet open, but I spent a delightful afternoon quite alone in the two great art galleries. One of these contained a remarkable collection of paintings by the Spanish masters – Velasquez, Zubaran, El Greco, Goya, and a great number whose names are rarely heard outside their native country. Most of these are normally either inaccessible in private houses or to all intents and purposes equally hidden in the obscure chapels of Spanish cathedrals. A series of four fantastic paintings by an anonymous artist of the eighteenth century particularly attracted me; they were named after the seasons, and represented, from a distance, female heads which, on closer examination, turned out to be composed entirely of ingeniously painted arrangements of the fruits and flowers of each quarter of the year; this, I suppose, is the ancestry from which are descended the picture-postcards one sees sometimes on stalls, of race-horses whose anatomy is curiously determined by the interlaced limbs of four or five nude female figures. The other gallery, which also was empty except for one very young and one very old priest, making a brisk tour side by side, was full of Spanish applied arts; beautiful carved Calvaries, reredoses, choir stalls; gold and silver pyxes, monstrances and tabernacles and communion plate; candlesticks and crucifixes – most of these lent from cathedral treasuries. There was also a gorgeous series of tapestries lent by the king from the Escurial. And, so far from suffering the bargain-sale scramble of a loan collection in London, one was able to walk round these superb galleries absolutely alone.

But the whole exhibition was like that. Tourists had so far not arrived in any appreciable quantities, and the Sevillians after sixteen years' preparation were bored with the whole business. There were elements of ill-feeling in their neglect. They considered that the price of admission was too high and that they had been unrighteously defrauded of the use of their favourite park. There was no organized boycott, but it just so happened that no Sevillians went to their exhibition. There was a model railway, with a miniature steam-engine, which took an empty train round and round the ground; there was an *Attracion* Park in which a great wheel revolved, empty; there were switch-backs and scenic railways on which empty cars swooped and swerved through breath-taking descents; there were silent rifle ranges with heaps of ammunition lying undischarged and mountains of bottles unbroken; in the evening the gardens were brilliantly illuminated; the trees were filled with electric-light bulbs in the shape of apples, oranges, and clusters of bananas; ingeniously concealed floodlamps made the lawns luminous and many coloured; electric lights were hidden under the water-lilies on the lake; illuminated fountains sparkled high in the air, like soundless and inexhaustible fireworks. It would have been a fascinating scene even in a Wembley crowd; on the night of my visit there was not another figure stirring anywhere; I felt as if I had achieved the Nonconformist ideal of being the only righteous soul saved in the universe; quite, quite alone in the whole of paradise. I suppose it really is not wholly gracious to emphasize this particular feature of the exhibition, as it can clearly not have come about by any deliberate intention of the organizers. To compliment them on it is somewhat like the polite painter who I once overheard, while being shown round the infinitely nurtured and tended garden of an acquaintance, congratulate his host on the excellence of his 'soft, mossy lawns'. Rather a touching paragraph in the prospectus said: 'In view of the large number of visitors expected at Seville throughout the Exposition, several new hotels and two garden-cities have been constructed...suited equally, in their variety, to the millionaire and to the most moderate purses ... Seville will accommodate some 25,000 visitors simultaneously throughout the Exposition.' It certainly merited the concurrence of 250,000, but I was very thankful that I saw it as I did, before anyone else arrived.

I had no meals on shore in Seville but sampled several vintages of Manzanilla in the cafés; it is a very dry species of sherry, served as a rule with a little piece of smoked boar's-head; the inferior brands taste like the smell of evening newspapers, but the best is very fine and delicate. There was a reception on the *Stella* for the Archbishop of Andalusia and various chaplains and officials; they drank glasses of champagne and ate iced cake and smoked cigars; conversation was impeded by our ignorance of Spanish and their ignorance of all other languages, but everyone smiled continuously and it had every evidence of being a success as a party; this, it may be remarked, happened just before luncheon.

Exigencies of the tide made it necessary for us to leave in the early afternoon of our second day. We turned, after prolonged and skilful manoeuvring, and sailed back down the river to the coast, crossing the bar into the Gulf of Cadiz at high tide that night. Early next morning we rounded Cape St Vincent. From then onwards, with a brief call at Lisbon, we headed straight up the Atlantic coast for England.

'I do not find Lisbon so pretty town as I have been tinking about,' remarked one of my Swedish friends as we leant over the rail, watching the lights of the harbour disappear behind us. He had lost heavily at the Casino, and I think that had embittered him. For me Lisbon was a very agreeable surprise. There is no European capital of any antiquity about which one hears so little; I know practically nobody else who has ever been there even for a day. And yet it is readily accessible; it has a romantic and honourable history intimately allied, if that is any commendation nowadays, with our own; a unique style of architecture, and inhabitants of marked racial peculiarities.

It lies in a beautiful natural harbour, where the river Tagus suddenly swells out into a great lake before narrowing again into the little bottle-necked mouth. The town is built on the side of a range of low hills, with domes and towers on most of the highest points; the water front is equalled only by that of Dublin in the purity of its architecture. It was built in the middle of the eighteenth century, after the demolition of the earlier buildings in the great earthquake. The central feature is the lovely Praça do Commercio, a square open on its fourth side to the water's edge, with a fine equestrian statue in the middle; behind this extends the Cidade Baixa, excellent eighteenth-century streets, rectangularly planned; behind them again lies the Rocio, a square known to generations of English sailors as 'Roly-Poly Square'; the great new boulevard, Avenida da Liberdade, runs from the Rocio to the northern extremity of the town, and on either side the eastern and western quarters rise on two densely populated hills.

Before luncheon I drove out with two fellow passengers to the Convent dos Jeronymos de Belem, a fine sixteenth-century building just outside the town on the coast road. This was my introduction to the Arte Manuelina – the style of architecture evolved in Portugal at the time of her commercial greatness. It is well described in the words of Baedeker as 'the fantastic style of the time of Emmanuel I the Great, a picturesque blend of late-Gothic, Moorish, and Renaissance features with *motifs* from the gorgeous edifices of the East Indies'. Belem is the only perfect example of this style in Lisbon, as buildings of this kind are naturally unsuited to withstand even the strains of their own weight, and all the others came hopelessly to grief in the great earthquake of 1755. It is a comic but not disagreeable manner of building, and antiquity has mellowed and refined the undue opulence of its decoration. The few attempts I saw to revive it in modern times seemed peculiarly infelicitous. It is the sort of architecture, one feels, that was never really intended to be built at all; it is a painter's and draughtsman's architecture, of the kind one sees in the background of northern sixteenth-century paintings and wood engravings, in which slender pillars, all fretted and twisted, support vast stretches of flamboyant fan-tracery; it is the sort of decoration one can imagine more easily in cast steel than in stone. Since 1834 this building has been converted into an orphanage, and the fabric seemed to have suffered somewhat in consequence; the elaborately carved stalls in the church were crumbling with dry rot. We went out into the cloisters; it was play-time, and hundreds of male orphans were tearing up and down, rolling each other in the gravel, kicking and hitting each other, and throwing small stones in each other's faces; the noise, reverberating through the vaulted roof, was deafening; our ears sang with it for half an hour afterwards; I trembled for the security of these fragile pinnacles, that intricate fretwork of carved stone. One of the orphans very politely conducted us round; he spoke English accurately, and was, it so happened, coal black. It is one of the interesting things about the Portuguese that the lower orders all show more or less marked negro characteristics. This is attributed to the extensive inbreeding in the Portuguese African colonies, and also to the policy, said to have been prosecuted by the great Pombal, of introducing a stud of negroes to repopulate the country after the ravages of the great earthquake.

I spent the afternoon driving about the town. It has not yet recovered from its earthquake, and most of the chief churches are left as ruins. In one of them, now used as a museum, I saw some interesting Peruvian mummies. At the top of a very high hill is the chapel of Nossa Senhora do Monte, much frequented by those who admire fine views, and also by women who wish to bear children, for in one of the side chapels is preserved an ancient stone seat which will cure the most stubborn case of barrenness, it is said, if the patient only sits on it for half a minute. There is also a very rich Jesuit church, called Sao Roque, well worth a visit on account of its frescoed ceiling, in which an almost unique trick of perspective has been employed; the plain vaulted roof is painted to represent elaborate architectural groining, with, between the false stone work, a series of frescoes conceived on quite different planes from their actual surface; a painting, as it were, of a painting. From all points of observation except one, the effect is barely intelligible; when, however, one stands in the centre of the floor, all the lines recede into their right places and an almost completely successful illusion is achieved. There is a false dome by Mantegna designed on a similar principle, and, of course, many compositions into which this kind of trick has been unobtrusively inserted, but I do not know of any example so complete and ingenious. It is only since the discovery of photography that perspective has ceased to be an art.

We sailed late that evening. Next day we were in a choppy sea, with a cold wind blowing from the shore, and that night we came into the Bay of Biscay; the ship developed a slow roll which caused serious discomfort to many. A great number of the passengers remained on deck during luncheon, nourishing themselves with dry biscuits and quarter-bottles of champagne. The roll went on undiminished until we rounded Cape Finisterre late in the afternoon.

In the channel news reached us by wireless of the results of the first day's count of the General Election; everyone prophesied a sweeping Labour victory, and the deepest gloom and apprehension settled upon the English passengers; many of the elder ones began wondering whether it would be wise to land.

The sea was quite calm now that we were out of the Bay of Biscay, but we ran into recurrent banks of fog which held up our progress; there was talk of our not getting in until late the next afternoon.

That evening there was a small party in the Captain's cabin, consisting of the officers off duty and two or three of the Scandinavian passengers and myself; we drank each other's health and exchanged invitations to visit each other in our countries. After a time I went out from the brightly lighted cabin on to the dark boat-deck. For the moment the night was clear and starry. I was carrying my champagne glass in my hand, and, for no good reason that I can now think of, I threw it out over the side, watched it hover for a moment in the air as it lost momentum and was caught by the wind, then saw it flutter and tumble into the swirl of water. This gesture, partly, I suppose, because it was of its own moment, spontaneous and made quite alone, in the dark, has become oddly important to me, and bound up with the turgid, indefinite feelings of home-coming.

For to return to one's own country, even after the shortest absence, is, in its way, an emotional business. I had left in the depth of winter and was coming back to late spring; then, if ever, England is still a lovely country. Tomorrow I should have a number of telephone calls to make; I should have to see my publishers about this book; I should have to order some new clothes; I should have to attend to a great heap of correspondence – bills and Press cuttings mostly, perhaps a few invitations.

I do not know on quite what terms we now deal with the emotions that were once called patriotism. Clearly we can feel very little martial ardour, or acquisitive ambition, or a pride of possession in other people's territory. And yet, although everything one most loves in one's own country seems only to be the survival of an age one has not oneself seen, and though all that one finds sympathetic and praiseworthy in one's own age seems barely represented at all in one's own country, there still remains a certain uncontaminated glory in the fact of race, in the very limits and circumscription of language and territorial boundary; so that one does not feel lost and isolated and self-sufficient. It seems to me that there is this fatal deficiency about all those exiles, of infinitely admirable capabilities, who, through preference or by force of untoward circumstances, have made their home outside the country of their birth; it is the same deficiency one finds in those who indulge their consciences with sectarian religious beliefs, or adopt eccentrically hygienic habits of life, or practise curious, newly classified vices; a deficiency in that whole cycle of rich experience which lies outside personal peculiarities and individual emotion.

So, suitably moralizing, I came near the end of my journey.

While I still stood on the boat-deck we ran into another belt of mist. The engines changed to slow and then to dead slow, and the fog-horn began dolefully sounding the half-minutes.

In twenty minutes we were clear again, and running under the stars at full speed.

I woke up several times in the night to hear the horn again sounding through the wet night air. It was a very dismal sound, premonitory, perhaps, of coming trouble, for Fortune is the least capricious of deities, and arranges things on the just and rigid system that no one shall be very happy for very long.

We came into harbour at Harwich early next morning; a special train was waiting for us; I lunched in London.